African American Autobiography and the Quest for Freedom

Recent Titles in
Contributions in Afro-American and African Studies

The Problem of Embodiment in Early African American Narrative
Katherine Fishburn

African Horizons: The Landscapes of African Fiction
Christine Loflin

Religious and Political Ethics in Africa: A Moral Inquiry
Harvey J. Sindima

Critical Perspectives on Postcolonial African Children's and Young
Adult Literature
Meena Khorana, editor

The Baltimore *Afro-American*: 1892–1950
Hayward Farrar

New Trends and Developments in African Religions
Peter B. Clarke, editor

Black Women Writers and the American Neo-Slave Narrative:
Femininity Unfettered
Elizabeth Ann Beaulieu

African Settings in Contemporary American Novels
Dave Kuhne

The Harlem Renaissance: The One and the Many
Mark Helbling

Willis Richardson, Forgotten Pioneer of African-American Drama
Christine Rauchfuss Gray

Critical Essays on Alice Walker
Ikenna Dieke, editor

Education and Independence: Education in South Africa,
1658–1988
Simphiwe A. Hlatshwayo

African American Autobiography —— and the —— Quest for Freedom

Roland L. Williams, Jr.

Contributions in Afro-American and African Studies, Number 191

GREENWOOD PRESS
Westport, Connecticut • London

Library of Congress Cataloging-in-Publication Data

Williams, Roland Leander.
    African American autobiography and the quest for freedom /
Roland L. Williams, Jr.
      p.   cm.—(Contributions in Afro-American and African studies,
ISSN 0069–9624 ; no. 191)
   Includes bibliographical references (p.   ) and index.
   ISBN 0–313–30585–4 (alk. paper)
    1. American prose literature—Afro-American authors—History and
criticism.   2. Autobiography—Afro-American authors.   3.
Afro-Americans—Education—History. I. Title. II. Series.
   PS366.A35 W55   2000
   810.9′492′000926073—dc21   99–28770

British Library Cataloguing in Publication Data is available.

Library of Congress Catalog Card Number: 99–28770
ISBN: 0–313–30585–4
ISSN: 0069–9624

First published in 2000

Greenwood Press, 88 Post Road West, Westport, CT 06881
An imprint of Greenwood Publishing Group, Inc.
www.greenwood.com

Printed in the United States of America

The paper used in this book complies with the
Permanent Paper Standard issued by the National
Information Standards Organization (Z39.48–1984).

10 9 8 7 6 5 4 3 2 1

To Andrea,
for her
love and laughter

"Keep, ancient lands, your storied pomp!" cries she
With silent lips. "Give me your tired, your poor,
Your huddled masses yearning to breathe free,
The wretched refuse of your teeming shore.
Send these, the homeless, tempest-tost to me,
I lift my lamp beside the golden door!"

— Emma Lazarus

Contents

Preface		xi
Acknowledgments		xv
1.	Dead Reckoning	1
2.	Blackwall Hitch	9
3.	Crow's Nest	41
4.	Jacob's Ladder	79
5.	Territorial Waters	115
Postscript		141
Sources		147
Index		153

Preface

My great-grandfather was born a slave. He arrived on a farm located near Allegheny Springs, Virginia. The date was April 9, 1865. That very same day, Robert E. Lee surrendered his sword to Ulysses S. Grant at Appomattox. The ceremony concluding the Civil War meant that my ancestor was destined to know more than slavery. By early summer, Union troops set him legally free to pursue his own happiness.

Named Charlie Williams, his father is unknown. He was raised by a devoted mother, Blanche, and a faithful stepfather, Roland, who worshiped learning and labored to see that their son attended school and acquired knowledge. Legend has it that he "thirsted for a complete education." During his youth, he studied hard. Eventually, he won entry into the Wayland Seminary in Washington, D.C., and graduated from the academy with honors.

In the familiar eyes of family and friends, my great-grandfather developed into a "giant." As well as marrying Mary Allen and raising twelve children with her, Charlie grew into an esteemed teacher. In a career that lasted over thirty years, he instructed a few generations of youths, looking to improve their lot. Most of the time, he worked in worn and paltry places. Still, he suffered neither despair nor weariness. He just kept on striving to make things better. On one occasion, he mustered the spirit to turn a shabby log cabin into a sturdy brick school. It would do much to have him recalled as "a mighty influence for good."

My great-grandfather passed away in the spring of 1917. His obituary proclaimed him "a burning and shining light." He remains a hero in my family. My father told me about him when I was a boy. Before I read a number of autobiographies, I believed that Charlie stood in a league of his own. Afterward, I teamed him with men like Booker T. Washington and Benjamin Franklin.

My opinion about my relative altered right after I discovered Franklin's *Autobiography* and Washington's *Up from Slavery*, plus other American autobiographies. Then, I began to consider his experience rather common in that it contains the stuff of legend in the land, present in the normal American life story that I read. It hit me that a personal history recollecting a rise in society pulled off through the use of learning sanctions the social ethos in a manner that renders it epic in nature, and it has marked a line of literature in the country. My great-grandfather's story embodies an unwritten version of the typical text. It reflects an attachment to a consensus swayed by a creed that has flooded each and every quarter of the country with the impression that all "men" are born equal, for everyone is endowed with a mind, like a garden, able to yield a fruitful crop through careful tending. Once I figured it out, Charlie became just one of many champions for me.

A comparative appraisal of African American life stories in writing, this study validates my understanding of my predecessor. It will challenge conventional wisdom. Since the rise of black studies programs, toward the end of the 1960s, leading critics have held black lives and letters in contradiction to the ways and writings of the mainstream culture. They have depicted black art as a racial strength transported from Africa and used in this country as a type of social resistance. The view fosters the notion that great black lives deviate in nature from heroic "American" tales. It suggests that such a life shores up extraneous social codes. By implication, black expression comes to have the import of a foreign tongue in the land.

The reasoning limits the scope of black books to a spot planted on a bank of the cultural mainstream.

My study endorses earlier images of black people in the country, conceived by critics like Sterling Brown. It inscribes the nation as a stage where blacks perform odd roles in a drama of "pioneers," progressive types akin to the Quakers, who rival "settlers," traditionalist sorts related to the Puritans. The civic performance has promoted the conception and cultivation of a convention domestically as meaningful as the *Odyssey* in Athens and the *Aeneid* in Rome. Complicated by color prejudice, circumstances have drawn everyone in the land to the novel convention, yet blacks to a special degree, proven by my great-grandfather in his actions and other blacks in their autobiographies, first in the work of slaves like Olaudah Equiano, Frederick Douglass, and Harriet Jacobs and continuing on through Colin Powell's story *My American Journey*. With their fellow Americans, blacks have shared and shaped the culture; it shows in their favorite styles as well as their statements.

Essentially, African Americans have become model members of a social development devoted to the task of seeing if a society based on the belief that people are born to enjoy free and easy lives through the application of learning can long endure. The country marks a break from past social orders bound by deference to a rigid hierarchy leaving the masses under the power of a few, lodged at the top of the social order. It has invited citizens to follow their conscience instead of custom. Accordingly, it has invoked the birth of a novel epic form. The drift of the new literary work charts the dreads and desires of human beings metaphorically drawn or driven, by an earthshaking movement, overboard from a watery ship, and suspended in thin air, twisting in the wind, above a lifeboat and the sea, until they chance to dive into the whirl of the shifting tides and there train themselves to swim solo with freedom and facility. Put in writing, the life of Charlie Williams, my great-grandfather, would serve as a classic example of the heroic narrative.

Acknowledgments

Thanks to the English department at Penn. Everyone in the graduate program contributed to this project, especially Robert Regan, Peter Conn, and Gregg Camfield. Thanks to Murray Beja. He gave me a start at the Ohio State University. Thanks to Temple University in general and the English department in particular. They picked me up when I was down. Thanks to my fellow Penn pal David Bradley. He cinched the deal. Thanks to Carolyn Karcher, Miles Orvell, and Phil Yannella. They rolled out the welcome wagon. Thanks to Walter Lomax. He opened his wallet. Thanks to my parents, Florence and Roland. They taught me to love learning. Thanks to my aunt Sis. She never let me go hungry. Thanks to George Butler, Deborah Whitford, and their crew at Greenwood Press. They went the distance with me. Thanks to Ike Newsum. He hooked me up with my soul mate. Thanks to Eric Williams. He has always truly been a great brother. Above all, thanks to Providence. When I least expected it, the force helped me to help myself. I pray that my effort pleases all of my backers and boosters, and serves to stir some broken spirits to beat the blues.

1

Dead Reckoning

Long have you timidly waded holding a plank by the shore,
Now I will you to be a bold swimmer,
To jump off in the midst of the sea, rise again, nod to me, shout,
And laughing dash with your hair.
                              —*Song of Myself*, Walt Whitman

A novel narrative floods the land from sea to shining sea. It hoists a heroic standard long unauthorized. Nationally, its motif elevates the story to an epic-in-prose level, heralding a new world order, very far removed from old models. Drawn from diverse sources, it has citizens seek to be remembered by posterity for clearing barriers to the enjoyment of liberty through the employment of learning. Waves of Americans have drafted it in assorted tones. The story paints "men" one by one born equal to the extent that each is endowed with a mind entitling everyone to pursue private interests unbridled by unnatural curbs. Its strokes forge a mode of expression bearing a theme crafted in a style that stands in tribute to the social ethos. In spirit, the narrative divulges the dream behind the land.

While far ahead, the story's end looms at the start. It leads off with a humble admission of a dynamic feat by the narrator whose experience forges the chief topic. The speaker has consummated a passage from a poor, old life to a rich, new one with the help of integrity plus industry and, above all, intelligence. He strives to serve the general American welfare by typecasting a personal triumph as an illustrative affirmation of a social paradigm. Soon in time, a mixed family history turns into a struggle for liberty won with skill. Properly, prosperity follows. The hero acquires lots of leisure and spends a good deal on public service. Pausing on the note with which it opens, the story holds, being trained to chart courses unforced by others works best for "men" since the world involves a state of flux where relying on prescribed practices will remain useful nearly as long as trying to stay still at sea will be viable.

A slave narrative such as the 1845 one printed by Frederick Douglass could be considered a prototype for the novel American epic. The designation would be logical. Yet, from another perspective, you could make an identical claim about the *Autobiography of Benjamin Franklin*. It is the same for many books by different Americans. Harriet Jacobs's slave narrative can be seen as a classic case, as well as, in a funny way, *Ruth Hall* by Fanny Fern. You could probably hang the tag on *Two Years before the Mast* by Richard Henry Dana. It would be hard to find Olaudah Equiano's record of his adventures less worthy.

This study stakes a claim for the slave narrative. Mostly, it aims to show how an effort to get to the bottom of the American mainstream could open and close with a look into a text from the African American literary genre, such as, for example, *The Interesting Narrative of the Life of Olaudah Equiano, or Gustavus Vassa, the African*. A past tendency to handle black discourse as countercultural art in academic circles, initiated by Black Nationalist critics late in the 1960s, motivated this project. By a comparative treatment of black and white texts, the following lines lead to the conclusion that a slave narrative personifies as true an American utterance as any words could possibly relate. Nonetheless, rather than function to grant black literature sole title to the status of paradigmatic letters, the ensuing survey merely means to establish that the slave narrative deserves to be celebrated for constituting one out of many modes of the same model of social thinking.

A pause to examine the wellsprings of the national outlook, placing the country near the crown of a rising tide in human evolution, operates to explain how the slave narrative, set at the head of an evolving tradition, reveals the main currents of a creed shoring up the national soul. The world passes from a historical stage in which warriors have reigned supreme and had their feats proclaimed by poets. As warfare has grown more pernicious through the intervention of science, it has migrated into less tenable terms and thrown a concurrent civilization into decline. The fact has become very hard to deny since 1945, when the United States dropped an atomic bomb on ground zero at Hiroshima. Warrior culture achieved its original great height over 5,000 years ago up the Nile in Africa at the moment that Menes the Warrior assembled Egypt into an empire and declared himself a pharaoh with a divine right to rule the province with might and arms. Romans and Russians, plus Greeks, Germans, and Ghanians, among other "men" across the planet, rose at one time or another into imperial powers under the leadership of a man-at-arms whom bards were bred to hail. During the Middle Ages, Europeans sought to convert the civilization into a kinder and gentler culture by a reformation of its soul through the design of chivalry, fundamentally a code bidding courtesy among soldiers, christened knights; still, after all was said and done, slaughter and subjugation, the cardinal habits of the tradition, survived, sanctioned by the idea that a chosen few were fated to rule the majority of a specific territory, in the mode of officers running a taut ship serviced by rowers unsuited to act under their own steam.

The psyche of the passing age has poured from epics. There is *Gilgamesh* from Mesopotamia. Scripted on tablets in cuneiform, after the first century of the second millennium prior to the birth of Christ, it survives as the oldest story on record. The long narrative poem professes to tell the history of a real king who ruled an extinct land,

once located around Nineveh, the capital of ancient
Assyria and the site of Mosul in modern Iraq. In a segment of the verse, Gilgamesh learns of a flood that proved
lethal to the known world, save a single household that took
shelter in an ark that outlasted the deluge and settled on a
mountain, pursuant to a supernatural decree. Deemed to a
degree divine, the hero hears of the events from an old survivor for whom he has long searched to question about
immortality. Throughout its body, the poem pictures Gilgamesh as a hothead hankering to cheat death and call the
shots in every instance for himself; by the moment that he
meets the flood survivor, he is a warrior who has
befriended the wild man Enkidu through a bout of wrestling, beheaded the monster Humbaba, and taken pleasure
in murdering a bull in lieu of marrying the goddess Ish-
tar. A great deal to Gilgamesh's dismay, the old survivor
ends his tale without telling him how to live forever; the
hero resolves that his fate lies beyond his control; he
resigns himself to the notion that he is fated to rule an
earthly kingdom with strength until higher powers say
that his time is up.

Homer and Virgil recited kindred warrior songs
in the *Odyssey* and the *Aeneid*. Invoking the Muse, Homer
refers to the hero Odysseus, as a pilgrim endowed with a
bag of tricks, counting cleverness in combat. It is apparent
that the tag is fitting in the wake of the reminiscence by the
Phaecian bard Demodocus regarding the herculean and
foxy role played by Odysseus in the construction of the
Wooden Horse and the conquest of the Trojan populace,
which prompts the Greek to tell the story of his adventures
over the last ten years since the final days of the war,
including an attack with the help of his soldiers on the
Ciconians, involving pillage and rape, before a clash with
the Cyclops, Polyphemus, leading to the blinding of the big,
brutish cave-dweller after Odysseus rams a spike in his
eye; the hero's fierce and crafty character is most evident
in the recovery of his throne in Ithaca, which he manages
by slipping into his palace incognito, clad as a beggar, and
so slaying his wife's suitors, everyone caught off guard.
All the while, starting with his release from the clutches of

the nymph Calypso, ordered by Zeus, to his return to Aeolus, originated by Poseidon, and his reunion with Penelope, orchestrated by Athena, Odysseus favors a pawn alternately manipulated by mercurial foes. Virgil too opens with a proclamation, designating Aeneas, the hero in his poem, a man of war shouldering a destiny, decided by celestial rulers, to launch the Roman empire. Eloquent stanzas of violent struggle and strife spin throughout the epic's body, culminating in the bloody battle with Turnus in which Aeneas kills his opponent. Time and again, volatile deities direct the action. It is apparent, once Aeneas forsakes Dido at the command of Jupiter, that honor for the hero lies in the acceptance that it is not his fate to chart the course of his own private life.

Every culture of the Old World has constructed such bellicose and fatalistic ballads. The number includes two narratives from the region of Africa below the Sahara: the *Mwindo* and the *Sundiata* epic. Hindu culture yielded the *Ramayana* and the *Mahabharata*. The old English tale starring *Beowulf* fits into this category. It is true likewise for the *Nibelungenlied* drawn from the wells of German lore. Additionally, Western civilization has produced the *Cantar de mio Cid* as well as the *Chanson de Roland*. Every one of the cited texts constitutes a moral compass that backs warfare and beckons "men" to see themselves in the world as passengers, as opposed to pilots, in their personal lives synonymous with practical posts in a convoy commissioned by lofty authorities.

The warrior epic tradition started on a downward spiral at the dusk of medievalism. The *Divina Commedia* from Dante signals the change in course. Stuffed by the late Medieval poet with scores of didactic meters, it praises free will and love while it limits violence to the punishment of vice. Dante asserts that "men" are not made to act as brutes; they are born to raise themselves to noble heights. A similar outlook resides in the *Faerie Queene* by Edmund Spenser; it grants humanity a mind to chart a sound course by choice; the effort, however, intent on praising chivalry in conjunction with Christianity, is checked time and again by a starring knight faithful in love but fierce in war. Praying to go the rest of the tradition one better, Milton created his *Paradise Lost*. Although, with the *Divina Commedia* and the *Faerie Queene*, Milton's composition means to spotlight spiritual peace more than physical strife, it concentrates on warfare between heaven and hell; still, it assigns people the power to devise their fortunes. The finely worded tales of Milton, Spenser, and Dante share a convention premised on grounds sinking out of fashion. A replacement was rising from an underground movement, seeing "men" born with the means to captain their fates. Gaining momentum since the hour that Johannes Gutenberg printed portions of the bible in 1453, by Milton's death in 1674, the rising trend was spilling out of the Old World and surfacing in the New World with renegades, who had crossed the Atlantic Ocean, clinging to words written with the wallop of John Bunyan's *Pilgrim's Progress* (1678), a reverie stationing the road to salvation under personal authority. The popularity of prosaic *Robinson Crusoe* (1719) by Daniel Defoe, about a shipwrecked sailor washed ashore an island where he has to improvise a practical mode of survival, proved that long narrative poems of fury and fatalism had lost ground to trailblazing narratives of freedom. By the Enlightenment, the poetic approach embodied essentially an anachronism.

In 1981, Mikhail Bakhtin noticed the sea change. "Whatever its origins, the epic as it has come down to us is an absolutely completed and finished generic form" (15), he said. Before Bakhtin, Alexander Pope saw that the old literary fashion was a dead issue. The eighteenth-century poet revealed his awareness by mocking the traditional epic in his *Rape of the Lock*. The poem succeeds by treating a filching of hair as an urgent call to arms.

The movement behind the eroded passion for the production of traditional epics ushered in the American Revolution. Folks everywhere around the country were moved to see themselves as pilots, rather than passengers, in the world. They came to believe that they were meant to discover good luck by gaining knowledge and using it. Increasingly, they thought, heroism rests more in finding freedom by becoming a skillful worker than in winning prestige by conquering others in the manner of a warrior skipper. Under the circumstances, the Old World habit of having poets salute legendary persons, seasoned in battle, could not pass muster. Given the mind emergent in America, rating people born to run their own affairs, only a personal confession, a song of the self, could harbor an epic charm. A long, unrhymed, meterless autobiography, recollecting a rise in society enabled by the benefit of intellectual talent and favoring conscience over custom, or innovation in lieu of tradition, was the perfect form for the public function.

Within the land, it is right that citizens have grown more familiar with the particulars of Benjamin Franklin's personal history than the details of George Washington's military career. The same can also be said about how the nation recalls President Abraham Lincoln more fondly than it does General Ulysses S. Grant. Warriors do not signify ideal characters in American thought. The consciousness that set the social mainstream in motion fosters an awe for efficient executives who transform themselves into public servants in contrast to bold braves who turn into powerful sovereigns. Issuing *Common Sense*, Thomas Paine caught the national drift with denials that anyone is born with a divine right to master others. The perception that buoys the nation maintains that prominence should not be won by force of arms; it ought to be earned by exercises of learning. Measured by the given moral yardstick, the trails blazed by Franklin and Lincoln amount to heroic track records.

The histories recounted in model African American autobiographies bear a significance similar to the lives of the local white heroes. Such black writings first appeared as slave narratives. The work of Equiano, Douglass, and Jacobs typify the early material. After the Civil War, the black books were tailored into freedmen's tales, telling of triumphs over tyranny, pulled off with smarts. A model of the second variety is Zora Neale Hurston's *Dust Tracks on a Road*, on top of Richard Wright's *Black Boy*, followed by Claude Brown's *Manchild in the Promised Land*, Maya Angelou's *I Know Why the Caged Bird Sings*, and *The Autobiography of Malcolm X*. Besides many others, each of the stated autobiographies has the weight of an epic in the country, for all of them uphold the social ethos.

The preceding remarks are confirmed in the coming chapters. In the very next one, entitled "Blackwall Hitch," a comparison of the autobiographies composed by Equiano and Franklin verifies that common talk about the human condition, representing an unusual belief system in global history, streams out of both texts equally, but scholarship has missed this in light of the fact that racism has cast black lives as unlikely reservoirs of local heroism. The third chapter, called "Crow's Nest," diagnoses Douglass's slave narrative in relation to Dana's memoir and spots proof that the nation has disposed African Americans to take on the dominant sense of decency. "Jacob's Ladder" ensues; it positions Jacobs's personal history with Fern's *Ruth Hall* to identify females in general and a slave girl in particular as fertile soil for the optimal flowering of a public idol. In "Territorial Waters," the final chapter, a survey takes place and winds up with African American stories moored in a sea of texts, proportionally around the country epic in character, yet distanced by permutations in tone.

2

Blackwall Hitch

In view of their fields and foundations, Olaudah Equiano, a product of Africa, and Benjamin Franklin, an offshoot of America, late in the eighteenth century had chances to walk in Philadelphia at the same hour. Although it is unlikely that their paths crossed and led them to talk, extant artifacts indicate that, in the local tongue with separate accents, the two could have engaged in dialogue upholding a common sense of "men." An archaeological approach to each of their personal narratives discloses the possibility. *The Interesting Narrative of the Life of Olaudah Equiano or Gustavus Vassa, the African* and *The Autobiography of Benjamin Franklin* taken together in context sound like a duet for a folk hero. Overflowing with matching tropes, aimed at a common audience, in comparison, the books reveal that their authors could have enjoyed a talk because they looked at "men" in the world a lot alike.

While it is true that from the 1760s until the mid 1780s Equiano and Franklin spent fewer of their days in Philadelphia than out of it, both men definitely could have met and spoken to one another in 1785. By early that autumn, each of them was around town. During the spring, profoundly "glad to see this favorite old [city] once more" (Equiano [1789] 1995, 186), Equiano had come ashore from a

British merchant ship out of London on which the ex-slave had earned his passage across the Atlantic Ocean by serving as a steward. It was May, the very month in which a year-old wish came true for Franklin. The white statesman received final approval from the country's new government to place in Thomas Jefferson's hands his diplomatic post in Paris and sail as soon as possible for his beloved home in the City of Brotherly Love. Hence, to great fanfare, Franklin arrived in town on September 14 and so landed in a position to encounter the African.

By then, they could have enjoyed a nice exchange because their patterns of thought had swung far from the grounds on which their elders had based their entire lives. If either one had failed to go the distance, in effect, to reject the mentality of his ancestors, any talk about "men" would have collapsed into an argument because their perspectives would have been bound to clash. The men had forefathers whose worldview revolved around the view that everyone is born to maintain a certain "station" in a set community; in sum, they both descended from folks who believed, overall, that human beings are born to play fixed parts in a rigid hierarchy. With age, their minds grew at odds with the climate of opinion that conditioned the thought of their progenitors; they gathered an enduring faith in the theory that the ranks of "men" are not fixed at birth. In a prudent society, the eighteenth-century figures came to reason, the stature of a "man" naturally stems from his schooling.

Equiano entered the world in "a charming fruitful vale, named Essaka," located in "one of the most remote and fertile" (34) jurisdictions in the kingdom of Benin during the dying days of a glorious era. Though now a poor part of southwestern Nigeria, in Equiano's lifetime the African territory had been legendary over 500 years for making handsome bronze and brass artwork crafted by a corps of sculptors authorized by sundry chiefs. Benin was a trading post that peaked in prestige during the sixteenth century, when the kingdom saw, as a sign of its success, the establishment of an enchanting court in a "twenty-five mile wide" capital city where huge residences "flanked" many "imposing boulevards and intersecting streets"

(Bennett [1962] 1984, 33). Until the province fell under British rule in 1897, it groomed its offspring to believe that "men" come to life with private missions, different in degree of importance. The vicinity, in sum, encouraged its inhabitants to suppose that everyone has a destination to reach before ever taking a single step.

Regarding "the manners and government" of his birthplace, Equiano recognized that the village "may serve as a specimen" (Equiano [1789] 1995, 34) of the Benin kingdom. Pious and productive, the natives in Essaka upheld a code of conduct that discounted individual choice. They were disposed to see every human life in the hands of "one Creator of all things" (41), who cast people into disparate roles. Their social ethos warranted doing little more than taking custom for granted. So, the people of the village daily labored to obey standards. In accord with tradition, men reigned over women, marriages were arranged, and war captives, along with social deviants, were enslaved. The biblical dictum "Remove not the ancient landmark, which thy fathers have set" (Proverbs 22.28) could have stood as a motto for the settlement. The natives were rather steadfast in their ways. They primed Equiano from birth to feel "*destined*" (Equiano 34) to walk in his father's footsteps and, in due course, to be crowned a tribal chief, entitled an Embrenche, who would obtain an indelible scar to wear on his forehead, signifying that his worth was a cut above that of most other villagers.

In configuration, Essaka was to Benin what the latter was to the larger region of West Africa; it was a microcosm. Between the ninth and sixteenth centuries, the area passed through a great period. Ghana, Mali, and Songhay, one after another, grew into dynamic empires that dominated trade in lucrative markets extending from the Senegal to the Nile and beyond. Each empire depended on a pyramidal structure that permitted a "chosen few" to rule the many, supposedly by birthright. Mali's epic *Sundiata* is epochal in this regard. Representing the hero as someone fated to be a warrior who would unite warring tribes into a mighty nation, the narrative captures the vision abroad; its narrator implores:

> But what can one do against destiny? Nothing.
> Man, under the influence of certain illusions,
> thinks he can alter the course which God has
> mapped out, but everything he does falls into
> a higher order which he barely understands.
> (Niane 1993, 22)

Again and again, the tale suggests that human beings lack the power to captain their own fates; it estimates that humans are merely made to act in response to external commands. The persuasion, disposed to allow a tolerance for inequality, threw West Africa open to the Atlantic slave trade that followed decline of the Dark Ages.

At any rate, a rigid hierarchical tradition pushed the kingdom of Great Britain, the homeland of Franklin's ancestors, into the international trade that linked Europe, Africa, and America into a terrible triangle of exchange in black bodies. In 1066, Great Britain instantly sprang into existence through the Norman invasion mandated by William the Conqueror; a faith in the Great Chain of Being, evident in *Beowulf*, laid the foundation for the country. Purportedly by birthright, kings were meant to reign at the very pinnacle of society, a notch below God. According to the scheme, at the base, the masses, deemed peasants, belonged beneath tiers of dukes and barons. Through the social system, the British learned to revere custom and frown upon change.

The estimate of propriety that pervaded the British realm surfaces in Franklin's memory of his forerunners' lives in Ecton, the rural village north of London in which his family dwelled for 300 years at least, before his father, named Josiah, "married young, and carried his Wife with three Children unto New England, about 1682" in order to practice openly a "Mode of Religion" (Franklin [1791] 1993, 31) utterly outlawed in the old county by the Crown and the Church. In Ecton, there prevailed a trust that a son is destined to step into his fathers' line of work. Thus, on nearly thirty acres, from their actual origins until the seventeenth century, the Franklins eked out a modest living "aided by the Smith's Business" to which "the eldest Son" was "always bred" (29). All of the boys served an apprenticeship in a trade involuntarily. Their conscience never won favor over custom. Custom urged them to take disparity in stride, to find some superior and others inferior due to their lineage.

Exposure to such backgrounds gave British men a mind to cut deals with West Africans for slaves to be sold in the New World. Great Britain embraced the enterprise late in the game. Several European nations, starting with Portugal in 1502 and later including Spain and Holland, beat Franklin's ancestral homeland to the punch. With the blessings of his countrymen, John Hawkins ushered Great Britain into the slave trade in the year 1562, when he shipped cargoes of captives bought from the vicinity of Equiano's forebears and sold them for a profit to Spaniards with a need for cheap labor on growing plantations in the West Indies, where Equiano would later suffer as a slave. Winthrop Jordan in his White *over Black* reports that Hawkins "made three voyages to Africa, the islands, and home." Success accented the first two trips; "the third met disaster at San Juan de Ulua when the Spanish attacked his ships," seized their crews and turned them over to officials of the Spanish Inquisition. Jordan trusts that "English vessels were not again active frequently in the slave trade until the next century" because the results of Hawkins's last venture unnerved them (Jordan 1969, 58-59). Nonetheless, "in 1663," reports David Brion Davis, "the Duke of York and a group of prominent shareholders, including the king [Charles II] himself, [launched] the Company of Royal Adventurers Trading in Africa, which [9] years later would be reorganized as the powerful Royal African Company" (Davis 1983, 131), a concern that would soon dominate the transatlantic traffic in slavery.

It was understandable for Englishmen to rush into the business with the resolve that some folks, like blacks, distinguished by a difference in color, are created to serve others. The attitude did not render Englishmen mentally different from the natives of Benin. Basically, through the seventeenth century, people akin to Franklin and Equiano shared a psychology that left them glad to practice human bondage. The outlook reflected the morals in circulation around Africa, Europe, and Asia before the start of the Enlightenment. It is worth noting that slavery originated as an exclusive rite of the population within the borders of neither Britain nor Benin. In civilizations throughout ancient history in the Old World, enslavement took place. Slavery was a fundamental part of life in Timbuktu, as it was in the municipalities Carthage and Rome in the wake of vital appearances in other cities from Egypt to Babylon. In fact, recalling ancient Greece's civilization, H. G. Wells observes in his *Outline of History* that "slavery was implicit in Greek life; men could conceive of neither comfort nor dignity without it" (Wells 1961, 270).

Aristotle's *Politics* in addition to Plato's *Republic* offers airings of conventional wisdom in the Old World up to the eighteenth century. Both philosophers assumed that some men are meant to inhabit lots situated rows below higher ones. Seeking to define the ideal society, in the guise of Socrates, Plato resolved that there are "naturally worse and naturally better" (Plato [ca. 380 B.C.] 1992, 107) human beings and and true justice demands that every citizen "practice one of the occupations" in the community "for which he is naturally best suited" (108). The thinker's regard for humanity licensed him to condone slavery. His fellow countryman, Aristotle accepts slavery, for he perceives it as an activity that conforms to how "a ruling element and a ruled" (Aristotle [unknown] 1971, 12) loom in each and every single aspect of nature. He professes a certainty that some have an inherent ability "to exercise forethought" (3) and as a result are fit to lord over others typically endowed with brute strength. In a good society, alleges Aristotle, brainy men rule brawny ones in accord with the cosmos.

Outside Sophist discourse, from philosophers like Protagoras, holding "a bias toward relativism" (Patterson 1991, 149), Orlando Patterson looking at "the valorization of personal liberty" in "Western civilization" (402) finds, among ancient world cultures, scarce faith in the concept of organic equality among various human beings. Patterson understands Aristotle's approval of slavery as an analytical posture made to save a master class; afterward, he regrets, "it has startled many, and no doubt [embarrassed a few] admirers of Aristotle," that *Politics* opens with a deliberation on the vital "role of slaves" (162) in society. Patterson remarks that Plato's *Republic*, in concert with Aristotle's treatise, backs slavery as it divides people into ranks of higher and lower talents for whom justice exists when everyone does what comes naturally to him (174), or, to put it otherwise, when all adhere, in the immortal words of William Shakespeare, "to the manner born." The scholar establishes that past social orders, including those of the Chinese, Celts, and even the Cherokees, subscribed to a belief system that sanctioned slavery. In every case, it was deemed honorable to treat inequality as a fact of life.

Taking certain individuals to be naturally inferior, antique cultures developed without any design to afford the average person an opportunity to rise above his or her parent's tier in society. Looking to improve one's lot seemed illogical to earlier men and women who fixed their coordinates according to the mandates invoked by the slavery-tolerant forums pervasive during earlier times around the globe. Before the advent of the eighteenth century even appeared on the horizon, from Mesopotamia to Mali, powerful empires arose devoid of institutions built to offer the lower echelons an equal opportunity to reach heights unapproached by their forerunners. The most common social structure everywhere instructed its inhabitants to accept their places at birth and keep them for the rest of their entire lives. Training centers were created and conserved with care, beginning, most likely, in Sumer and, later, emerging in Egypt (Roberts 1993, 40-44, 55-56), but they served simply to aid aristocracies administered by bureaucracies committed to saving the status quo; it was certainly the function of the Egyptian Mystery system, a secret order dedicated to initiating select neophytes into the inner circles of power in the grand ancient African civilization. All such institutions talked men and women into taking their social orders to be essentially, in effect, the kind of cultural organization that was well described by the English writer H. G. Wells as "*a community of faith and obedience*" or a human civilization strictly arranged in opposition to the practice of individual choice (Wells 1961, 588).[1]

Old communities could be described as tight ships. They were run by men (titled, e.g., pharaoh, emperor, or king) who acted like an incontestable captain appointed in the stead of a higher power.[2] With assistance from hands molded to serve in capacities comparable to those of naval lieutenants and petty officers, the rulers riveted their social orders to courses charted by tradition. The normal routine programmed most people to occupy themselves as robots reminiscent of rowers chained to a ship and needed to keep the craft in motion. Through lips belonging to an initial victim of the latter predicament, the first cry for freedom must have passed and aroused others similarly situated.

Patterson takes the previous statement seriously. He asks, "Who were the first persons to get the unusual idea that being free was not only a value to be cherished but the most important thing that someone could possess?" He answers, "in a word: slaves." Moreover, he contends,

---

1. The italics are Wells's own. His *Outline of History* contains a thesis with which I strongly agree. It suggests that the "modern state" is a revolutionary innovation in world history resting on the belief that an informed and free community constitutes the best of all possible worlds. Bouts of racism, however, mar the book. For example, there is a moment when the author blindly argues that "the most settled civilized peoples" on the planet "were originally in most cases dark-white Caucasians" (583). Wells saw that a stream of consciousness dedicated to human rights has been evolving in the world, but he, being a product of a racist time and place, could not imagine how black Africans played vital parts in human progress. Apparently, he found the Sphinx's Negroid features insignificant with regard to how the people who had it built must have looked. Wells was committed to a whitewash of history, crediting human progress to whites or dark whites, not blacks or light blacks. Research indicates that blacks and light blacks founded Egypt and so Western civilization. 5000 years of invasions and immigrations make things look otherwise. Consider how the color of America has changed and is changing; 500 years ago, "red" men lived throughout the territory and today they are scare. For a better understanding of blacks in Egypt and early world history, see *The African Origin of Civilization* (L. Hill, 1974) by Cheikh Anta Diop, *Black Athena* (Rutgers University Press, 1987) by Martin Bernal, *Blacks in Antiquity* (Belnap Press, 1970) by Frank Snowden, and *An Enchanting Darkness* (Michigan State Press, 1993) by Dennis Hickey and Kenneth Wylie.

2. Wells notes that "god-kings or kings under gods" cemented "primitive civilizations" (585).

"Freedom began its career as a social value in the [awful] yearning of the slave to negate what, for him or her, and for nonslaves, was a peculiarly inhuman condition" (9). He suspects that as slavery evolved from its conception, it worsened and extended interest in abolitionism.

In the *African*,[3] slavery in the New World strikes Equiano as "a new refinement in cruelty" (58), once he experiences it, and he quickly wants to abolish it. But in his village, before his own kidnapping and enslavement, he takes slavery for granted within his own household. Equiano illustrates that his father was an eminent warrior chief whose word by custom was law in his own home, and hence the elder had the authority to exercise great control over the affairs of "a numerous family" as well as "many slaves" (46). Warnings about marauders who travel with large sacks to catch unsuspecting children and toss them into bondage cause the not much more than eleven-year-old boy Equiano concerned about being unfortunate enough to be snatched by the raiders, but older villagers assure him that he is slated for good luck; they raise him to aim to live "after the manner of [their] greatest warriors" (47). The environment in his birthplace solicited him in sum to imagine himself converting into a local hero in command of many underlings. His personal history affirms that the Essaka settlement prompted bondage to represent, in his eyes, a calling meant for people unlike him.

Slavery never genuinely offends Equiano until he beholds himself trapped inside it. He goes unbothered by his father's authority to order a man to hand the ruling chiefs his slave, as if the captive were just a form of dumb livestock, forfeited as a fine for violating a tribal village ordinance. During his boyhood in Essaka, Equiano never minds that adulterous wives (no more contemptible than Hester Prynne) are cast into slavery, if not killed, while their mates indulge in polygamy. Yet, once he is seized, besides his sister, by the marauders, numbering "two men and a woman" (47), he wants to condemn their actions. Poignantly, being gagged and sacked stops Equiano from

---

3. Henceforth, I refer to the slave narrative as the *African* for short.

protesting. His wish to object, at any rate, grows stronger during the following day after a night spent in a huddle with his sibling; he recounts that "my sister and I were then separated" (48). Subsequently, alone, he is sold to several African masters whom he serves all together for just a few months and meanwhile sways between moments of misery and mortification, despite, as a rule, receiving kind treatment from the slaveholders who hold him, including a fine goldsmith and a wealthy widow, whose manners invite him to regard himself as a junior family member. Clearly, while still a child, Equiano accepted bondage until his own entry into it assured him that it is a wretched business; it plagues human life with gloom.

The impact of the social consciousness that steered premodern African cultures and in the process sanctioned human mastery over others eluded Equiano's full grasp. He would most likely have had to live another 100 years or so in order to comprehend the frame of mind's effect on the region. Had he possessed a chance to look back from a 20th-century vista and witness his country's subsisting in poverty, Equiano would have been able to recognize that the reigning ethos of the past loaded the territory with innumerable chiefs readily tempted by the spoils of the slave trade and it thereby metamorphosed the area into a setting approximating "a huge slave corral" (Quarles 1987, 21) where "it was not at all unusual for an African to sell an African today and to be captured and [peddled] himself tomorrow" (Bennett 47). Armed with the later awareness, Equiano would have realized that "from time immemorial men in Africa" (Quarles 21) tolerated slavery, and it laid the continent open to ruin. Realistically, though, from his place in history, Equiano could just theorize from his experience that, during his time, a spread of black slavers, "sable destroyers of human rights" (Equiano 50), backed by tradition, injured their black neighbors rather severely through a willingness to enslave and sell them to foreign merchants prone to add "fresh horrors" to a very savage enterprise with "no advantage to atone for it" (58).

While Olaudah Equiano's enslavement led him to view his countrymen's rites with a critical eye, for he had subscribed to their mentality in his early boyhood, he yet and still never had a reason to deem himself irrational in comparison with thinkers like Franklin. Throughout the bulk of the latter's life, he lacked the conviction to proclaim it "self-evident" that "all men are created equal." For, beyond one score and ten years,[4] Franklin manifested a tendency to entertain ideas well in harmony with the sentiments of the African slavers who subjected Equiano to the evils of the Atlantic slave trade. During Franklin's own life, the famous "founding father" routinely kept a bit of the African diaspora, unloaded in Pennsylvania by slave traders, enslaved in his Philadelphia household. In fact, he reached old age before he deemed it right for him to issue an outcry against slavery.

Fleeing New England, Franklin first arrived in the City of Brotherly Love at 17 years of age with a belief that "men" stand below God, above animals, and separate and unequal at birth. A measure of his perspective most likely arose from his brief exposure to the Boston Grammar School expected to prepare boys for a puritanical ministry in New England. Like Robinson Crusoe's dad, Franklin's father directed him to fathom himself born to a post that only a fool would abandon. On the whole, his upbringing instilled in him a mind to count different people as gradations of humanity. In 1728, imagining the world as a complex of higher and lower beings, Franklin professed in his "Articles of Belief and Acts of Religion" that "Man is not the most perfect Being but One, rather that as there are many Degrees of Beings his Inferior, so there are many Degrees of Beings superior to him" (1987, 83).

---

4. In "Introduction: The Life of Benjamin Franklin," appearing in the Bedford Books edition of *The Autobiography of Benjamin Franklin* (1993), Louis P. Masur reports, "For more than thirty years, [Franklin owned] several slaves who served mainly as household servants" (13). *Freedom by Degrees*, (OUP, 1991), coauthored by Gary Nash and Jean R. Soderlund, offers a more informative account of Franklin as a slaveholder. According to the authors, Franklin "first purchased slaves" most likely "in the late 1740s" (ix). Another telling report comes in the work of Claude-Anne Lopez and Eugenia W. Herbert, entitled *The Private Franklin*. The book's authors relate, "The fact is that Franklin himself kept slaves for over thirty years." His last one died, they reveal, in 1781 (1975, 292).

Earlier, masked as an immigrant named Silence Dogood, he echoed Plato's conviction that everyone comes to life with a job to do for his society; as Franklin wrote, "It is undoubtedly the Duty of all Persons to serve the Country they live in, according to their Abilities" (9). At twenty-seven, under the guise of a contributor to the *Pennsylvania Gazette* named Blackamore, Franklin painted himself as an "ordinary Mechanick," prayed that he might "always have the Grace to know [his] self and [his] Station," and argued that a person who tries to detach himself from his class, that is, "his natural Sphere," his proper element, his predestined station, happens to be a terribly ridiculous and contemptible person (1987, 219-20).

Knowing the psychological baggage with which Franklin commenced his career in the City of Brotherly Love makes it no wonder that he kept slaves, with names used for pets (for example, King, Jemima, and Othello), once he prospered in the printing trade and so could afford to hire cheap labor do the dirty work around his house. Franklin was a man of his time and place. "In an age infused with the presuppositions of the Chain of Being," Jordan plainly points out in *White over Black*, "it was fatally easy to [see] Europeans and the rest of mankind as constituting a Great Chain of Color" (254). That was the case for Franklin. It may come as a shock. Still, his mind was furnished with an inclination to divide humans on a scale into higher and lower classes based on the color of their skins.

In 1751, pondering how the population in American society might best increase, he advocated taking steps to turn the colonies into colossal preserves for propagating "purely white People" whose present "Number" on the planet, he disclosed, "is proportionably very small." He remarked that Englishmen "make the principal Body of White People on the Face of the Earth," and Franklin rued that

> *Africa* is black or tawny. *Asia* is chiefly tawny.
> *America* (exclusive of the new Comers) wholly
> so. And in *Europe*, the *Spaniards*, *Italians*,
> *French*, *Russians* and *Swedes*, are generally of

> what we call a swarthy Complexion; as are the
> *Germans* also. (1987, 367)

More importantly, Franklin suggested that the exclusion of all "Blacks and Tawneys" from "this Side of our Globe" would dispose the region to "reflect a brighter Light" (1987, 367-74) to a candid world. His position made it clear that he felt quite estranged from dark people. He judged them unwarranted in the New World, where, he supposed, the rule was destined to be that "no Man continues long a Labourer for others . . . [or] continues long a Journeyman to a Trade," but each in due course "sets up for himself" (369). In his eyes, only a select few with white skin tones harbored the right stuff to pass muster in North America.

Franklin's private sense that inherited differences in color augur inherent distinctions in human character contradicted the talk of the town in Philadelphia and, evermore so, in every other borough sprouting along the seaboard from which the country would evolve. All around men and women were given to speaking of the world as if it were in relation to them as pliant as the sea for a seasoned swimmer. They fondly insisted that humans stand out in the universe, for they alone have the power to chart their courses in life. Few doubted that disparities among "men" issue from the way in which their minds have been cultivated. With training and interest, eighteen-century American people would say, everyone could fare swimmingly.

The man in the street sounded like William Penn. Reacting to widespread intolerance in his native England, Philadelphia's founder exclaimed that people ought to let their conscience, instead of custom, guide them. Penn granted them the privilege, for, as a devout Quaker, he believed that "men" are born with an "inner light," which, though it requires triggering to work, once ignited, can lead to happy endings. The world's maker, Penn thought, "has made of one blood all nations" (Tolles 1957, 73). Plus, he avowed, it has given humans an intellect with which "to discern things and their differences, so as to assert or deny from evidences and reasons proper to each," and whenever a society prevents individuals from abiding by their own criterion, the restriction amounts to slavery, violates the "right of liberty, and so perverts the whole order of nature" (73); in a sense, Penn inferred that all Homo sapiens have a natural right to sink or swim by their own measures. Therefore, he pulled for equality far before Franklin's birth. He justified his outlook with the remark that "Reason, like the sun, is common to all, and 'tis for want of examining all by the same light and [dial] that we are not all of the same mind, for all have it to that end, though all do not use it so" (191). With tracts such as *The Great Case of Liberty of Conscience*, released in 1670, Penn, who envisioned Philadelphia as a "Holy Experiment" meant to nurture tolerance and fairness, helped to implant in the Western Hemisphere a way of talking about the human condition destined to foment the American Revolution in the late eighteenth century.

The discourse was nothing new under the sun. It issued from a stream of consciousness long abroad in the world. A faith, in spirit, it opposed checks on choice. It granted people an even birthright to determine their own direction in life. The creed rated blind obedience to custom beyond prudence. Dating back to the dawn of man-made rigid hierarchies, it was taken up by the Israelites who slaved in ancient Egypt and later by their heirs whom Hitler and his henchmen sought to exterminate; early Christians subject to being fed to wild animals in imperial Rome adopted the belief; and, English Nonconformists pilloried during the Georgian era embraced it, too. A great reverence attended each declaration of the underground trust, but it never prevailed in a political contest to become a civil raison d'etre before Christopher Columbus hit upon the Bahamas and touched off a chain of events that stripped convention away from America and in the interim cleared grounds for the building of American society.

Thomas Jefferson witnessed the conviction as the force that moved the multitude to act in concert and stage a revolt against British rule. Further, the Virginia squire realized that the credence under study arose from a history of compression endured in underground channels over the globe. Correspondence to Henry Lee proves that Jefferson deemed the authority for the Declaration of Independence to hinge readily "on the harmonizing sentiments of the day" (Jefferson 1984, 1501). The vox populi, he hinted ex post facto, cried against treating men as unequals upon birth; it leaked, he sustained, a profound sense that most people are not born like horses "with saddles on their backs, nor a favored few," as riders with boots and spurs on their feet, "ready to ride them" (1517) by divine decree. Jefferson ascertained in American discourse a confidence that "men" are made alike and so merit mutual respect.

Jefferson dreamed that the nation would progress into a fortress against a global storm of tyranny driven by ignorance and superstition about "men" and their powers. In the best of all possible worlds, which he hoped that the nation would become, a natural gentry is due to flourish, he posed. Mainly, he wished for the nation to replace what he imagined as the usual state, a culture skirted by artificial boundaries barring true and talented parties from achieving prominence. His formula for success consisted of a simple equation pointing to learning as the key. Jefferson insists in a letter to George Wythe, "No other sure foundation can be devised, [to assure] freedom and happiness," than "the diffusion of knowledge among the people." In the note, the author encourages Wythe to push for "a crusade against ignorance," plead for a public school system, and prove to the citizens "that the tax which will be paid for this purpose is not more than the thousandth part of what will be paid" (Peterson 1981, 399-400) to the sequence of dictators and demagogues who are likely to take charge in the absence of a public educational system open to all citizens.

Unorthodox Old World sages like Locke, Voltaire, and Kant, who rejected conformity and respected conduct guided by mental cultivation, talked up the Enlightenment and had a direct influence on the original American imagination. From Locke, for example, Jefferson and his fellows gathered that the "state all men are naturally in" constitutes a condition of "perfect freedom" to do "as they think fit, within the bounds of the law of nature, without asking leave, or depending upon the will of any other man" (Kramnick 1995, 395). Voltaire supplied Americans with proof that, although "men, in the enjoyment of their natural faculties, are equal" (Kramnick 417), since each one has a mind that grows very powerful with care, "the dominion of custom" has wrongly been "much more extensive than that of nature" (375) and so "little else than a long succession" (371) of ugly societies have stamped history. Kant alerted the land that bad situations marking past civilizations stemming from "statutes and formulas," constituting awful "fetters" (Kramnick 2) in nature, are rendered far too transparent a corruption to keep minds in check in a culture that prizes cultivating reason. Peace will reign, said Kant, in league with Locke and Voltaire, anytime everyone is empowered to use "his understanding without direction from another" (1).

Such intellectuals readied Americans to hail a heroic type outcast on Old World shores. An immigrant from France, St. John de Crevecoeur caught their drift. Identifying "men" as beings akin to plants, inclined to simulate "the peculiar soil and exposition in which they grow," he believed that Americans had derived from benevolent surroundings a devotion to a "new mode of life" fated to "one day cause great changes in the world" ([1782] 1986, 70). He dressed an ideal citizen in the garb of a festive freeholder "animated with the spirit of an industry which is unfettered and unrestrained, because [he] works for himself" (67). A shining star in the land, conveyed Crevecoeur, is a "man" who has climbed in his neighbors' eyes by acquiring and applying some prowess in order to meet his private needs and wants.

Within that climate of opinion, a tale written to record a gallant escape from tyranny leading to prosperity through the use of savvy was ripe for applause. The story was liable to strike a responsive chord because it lent credit to the social ethos. Its plot constituted bona fide proof that people have a gift for enjoying freedom and ease. In the land, it amounted to an epic story. Franklin might have understood this when he wrote his *Autobiography*. If not, he nevertheless managed to fashion a personal history that sanctioned the faith of his era and so became legendary.

Franklin's autobiography revolves around a flight from tyranny. It opens with a humble introduction hoping that the reader will find it useful to know how he passed from agony to ecstasy. In the ensuing account, he reports that his father, Josiah, was a Nonconformist who ran from England to practice his "Mode of Religion with Freedom" ([1791] 1993, 31), yet comes to expect blind obedience from his son. Josiah refuses to indulge the poor boy's "strong Inclination for the Sea." It does not matter that young Franklin has spent much of his time in Boston waterways and "learnt early to swim well, & to manage Boats" (33); his father denies him the liberty to lead the sailor's life for which he longs. Instead, Franklin's father forces him to work against his will in the family business. "A Thirst for Knowledge" (36), though, which Franklin assiduously strives to quench, incrementally empowers him to heed his own wishes. Subsequent moments in the narrative credit the pursuit of learning for his success.

Franklin's life hits rock bottom before it starts to veer toward smooth sailing. The low point for him arrives once his father, noticing that he has grown bookish, wants to make him "a Printer" (36) to keep his mind off poetry (deemed a frivolous pursuit) and thus binds him to serve as an apprentice in his brother's shop. To his dismay, James, his sibling, belittles and beats him; "Tho' a Brother," the narrator says, "he considered himself as my Master" (41). Luckily, Franklin becomes a diligent student of printing on the job and writing in his spare time. The two skills prove to be "a great Use to [him] in the Course of [his] Life." He looks back and sees them as "a principal Means of [his] Advancement" (37). First of all, they clearly render him wise enough to outwit his brother and break the bond that has tied him to the other's business; then, the skills qualify him to set up his own print shop in Philadelphia and corner the local market in the middle of producing his popular *Poor Richard's Almanac*; and, pretty materially, they enable him to compose and print the pamphlet entitled, "The Nature and Necessity of a Paper Currency," which wins him an exclusive contract "printing the Money" for Pennsylvania. It proves "a very profitable Jobb" (77); in the wake of it, he goes on "swimmingly" (78); his success leaves him in charge of his time, and he elects to contribute a large sum of it to public service.

In the letter of Benjamin Vaughan, which appears in the *Autobiography*, Franklin's story "is connected with the detail of the manners and situation of a *rising* people." In essence, Vaughan sees, it catches the American spirit. He thinks that Franklin's experience reveals how "the thing is in many a man's private power" to map out a plan by which to become "considerable" in the world through "*self-education*" ([1791] 1993, 82-83). Addressing his confidant Franklin, Vaughan says, "You prove how little necessary all origin is to happiness, virtue, or greatness" (83). Franklin's friend perceived that his recollection was sure to draw praise from his peers for dignifying their social faith, dedicated to the proposition that "all men" are born to gain self-sufficient lives through the pursuit of knowledge.

Contemporary black Americans were quick to toast a story that went the way that Vaughan saw Franklin's tale going. As members of American society, the blacks had been swayed by the prevailing current of thought as much as anyone and, to a remarkable degree, more than others. Their elders had arrived on the country's eastern shores as indentured servants in Jamestown during the settlement's second decade, in the year before the Pilgrim's *Mayflower* landed at Plymouth Rock. For nearly two generations, their ancestors had stood legally equal to white workers, whose American odyssey had commenced with indentured servitude.[5] Together with whites, in good faith, early black Americans toiled hoping to gain a decent chance to fend for themselves and prosper at the conclusion of four-to-seven-year contracts. Until the 1660s, under the law, black Americans were free to set their sights on reaching great heights. But, the rules changed for them, as Virginia and

---

5. In *Native and Strangers*, its author, Leonard Dinnerstein, writes, "It has been estimated that at least half, and perhaps two thirds, of all the white laborers in the colonies before the American Revolution arrived there as indentured servants" (13).

its neighboring provinces, one after another, enacted legislation sentencing blacks to slavery for life. In return, black people were pressed to gauge discourse about "men" being born for freedom as sacred speech.

Beginning no later than the year 1661, blacks sent hundreds of petitions to colonial authorities. In essence, the appeals verified that black folk were attuned to "the harmonizing sentiments of the day" (Jefferson 1984, 1501). The first one on record comes from a free, black couple seeking to adopt an orphan boy and secure his freedom. Every one of the pleas portrays individual liberty as a proper condition for human beings. By the eve of the American Revolution, a petition resolved that slavery is a "deplorable state" from which "*as men*, [blacks] have a natural right to" gain relief. One plea spelled out an apprehension that blacks "have in common with all other men a naturel right to [their] freedoms without Being depriv'd of them by [their] fellow men as [they] are a freeborn Pepel and have never forfeited this Blessing by aney compact" (Aptheker 1951, 1-9).

Blacks displayed an awe for the principles behind the colonial revolt against the British Crown. They made their feelings known through a series of slave rebellions. During 1663, a traitor exposed and thus had crushed a plot involving enslaved blacks and indentured whites eager to free themselves from their masters in Virginia. Hysteria seized New York in 1712 when "a serious uprising" by a band of black slaves spun into violent clashes between them and their bosses and left many dead on both sides. Writing to her husband, in 1774, Abigail Adams fretted "the discovery of a fairly widespread plot for rebellion among the [black] slaves of Boston" (Aptheker 1964, 15-23) and Herbert Aptheker notes that she closed her letter with the following reflection:

> I wish most sincerely there was not a slave in the province; it always appeared a most [unfair] scheme to me to fight ourselves for what we are daily robbing and plundering from those who have as good a right to freedom as we have. (1964, 23)

It is sound to say that her worldview harmonized with that of black Crispus Attucks, who, crying for freedom, was shot during the Boston Massacre and became the very first person to die for American independence.

As well as Jefferson or Franklin, blacks in early America expressed a certainty that success springs from learning. Undeniable proof lies in a 1787 petition written by free black people desiring equal access to learning for their children in the city of Boston, which was denied. Masterminded by Prince Hall, a preacher who had served as a patriot in the American Revolution, the document depicts the blacks as honest taxpayers who suffer fright because custom bars their children from studying in the schools. They find themselves under "a great grievance," since, in their eyes, "we, therefore, must fear for our rising offspring to see them in ignorance in a land of gospel light" (Aptheker 1964, 19). The text concludes with a prayer for the state government to judge it wise that "provision may be made for the education" (20) of black youngsters in the city.

Two years later, before Franklin's *Autobiography* was done, Equiano's *African* appeared in print with a sure appeal. The slave narrative champions the philosophy that animated early African Americans. It represents "men" in their natural state mirroring discrete figures at sea free to sink or swim depending on their knowledge of a way to sustain themselves. Everyone, it relates, comes to life with an "inner light," a particular ray of reason, ignited by encouragement and exercise; or, perhaps, more aptly put, the endowment is enlivened by a process comparable to how fair sunshine and fertile soil stir seeds to sprout into flowers. The motif in Equiano's story bears a visible resemblance to the theme in Franklin's narrative. Like the white text, the black one assumes epic proportions by featuring a hero who makes use of learning to improve his lot in life.

In the *African*, the main character grows to parallel a seasoned swimmer. For him, the development marks a radical rise in stature, very well illustrated, in the wake of a humble introduction that christens Equiano's memoir "the history of neither a saint, a hero, nor a tyrant" but, instead, the saga of someone who has known few things "which have not happened to many" ([1789] 1995, 33). The trailing reminiscence of his family casts his father in the mold of a man without an inclination to let his boy choose his own career; the older man seems bent on having his son follow in his footsteps. But whether or not his father might have caved in to Equiano's wishes, if the youth had wished to march to the beat of a different drummer, stays open to debate, for the kidnappers who snatch him from his village, end his contact with his family. Swept into slavery, he falls into a predicament similar to the plight of an empty sack buffeted by rough surfs in between bouts of being snared and subdued by transient sailors. He lives grimly at the mercy of others until he gains some useful knowledge.

First of all, learning to speak the tongue from kind American sailors such as Dick Baker and Daniel Queen gives him some say in his life; it helps him to understand ships and crews, besides other things, like snowflakes. By diligent study, Equiano transforms himself into an able seaman indispensable to a deft skipper. His ability draws Robert King's goodwill and moves the Quaker to engage Equiano and advance his education after Captain Michael Paschal has cut him loose. King affords him a chance to master the art of trade. Taking full advantage of the opportunity, Equiano soon goes into business for himself on the side. He profits and saves enough to purchase his independence in 1766. From that point, he obtains posts that carry him to shores from Nicaragua to Turkey in addition to the North Pole. Meanwhile, he plunges into the abolitionist movement and rounds into a resolute member.

The ties uniting the *African* and the *Autobiography* are unmistakable. Equiano's tale, like Franklin's story, has a humble introduction, followed by a family history, a reminiscence of dreadful tyranny, and a remembrance of ambitious learning. The two narratives progress to a disclosure of rewarded diligence, succeeded by an exercise of freedom for the public's good. Long, episodic forms, both books render the world as a state of flux where security emanates from learning. The hero in both cases frees himself from dire straits through the use of knowledge. Each one valorizes the talk of the town in eighteenth-century American society.

These findings decline to mandate the conclusion that the private histories of Franklin and Equiano survive without a shade of difference between them. For historical reasons, their autobiographies differ in tone. Their pitches vary to the degree that dialects of a language diverge. The contrast issues from a paradoxical pattern of thought that might well be dubbed "the Blackwall Hitch," a thick knot of reasoning, encompassing an erroneous idea of people with African roots. In principle, the problematic interpretation classified blacks as beings inferior to whites. It endorsed the doctrine that they are unfit for freedom since they lack the brains to benefit themselves by being their own bosses. Under its influence, black discourse, in sympathy with Equiano's *African*, came to express a peculiar touch of irony, setting it apart.

Europeans imported the false consciousness of blacks out of their Old World homes. It was forged by the labors of their ancestors to explain the physical variations between themselves and African people whom they began to met in the wake of their awakening from the slumber of the Middle Ages. Franklin exhibited an attachment to the Blackwall Hitch when he cottoned to own himself slaves. Adherents to the perspective found it arduous to consider blacks more than three-fifths of a white in worth since they were prone to regard the others as creatures related to monkeys lacking the ability to deliberate. David Hume betrayed a solid fidelity to the evaluation in his essay "Of National Characters," where he confides:

> I am apt to suspect the negroes . . . to be naturally inferior to the whites. There never was a civilized nation of any other complexion than white, or even any individual eminent either in action or speculation. . . . In Jamaica, indeed they talk of one negro as a man of parts and learning; but 'tis likely he is admired for

> very slender accomplishments, like a parrot
> who speaks a few words plainly. (Kramnick 629)

Hume's conviction alleges that blacks suffer from a lack of intelligence. His position was supported by Kant, who opined that "the [African people] have by nature no feeling that rises above the trifling." To this thinker, the bodily distinctions between whites and blacks are tied to "mental capacities," and being "black from head to foot" translates into "a clear proof" of stupidity (Kramnick 638-39).

The Blackwall Hitch induced Jefferson to consider blacks as "not men." It made it possible for him to enslave them and yet feel enlightened. Following the American Revolution and prior an outbreak of rumors about his romance with a female slave named Sally Hemings,[6] Jefferson professed that "nature has made" some huge differences between blacks and whites, and one of them is a "superior beauty" possessed by whites, which arises from their blushing cheeks and beautifully "flowing hair." White features, Jefferson swore, eclipsed each and every sort of black endowment, but mental properties evinced the most striking deviation. He mused that black lives involve "more of sensation than reflection." Jefferson said, "Comparing them by faculties of memory, reason, and imagination, it appears to me, that in memory they are equal to whites; in reason much inferior, as I think one could scarcely be found capable of tracing and [taking in] the investigations of Euclid; and that in imagination they are dull, tasteless, and anomalous." He clung to the suspicion that "nature has been less bountiful to [blacks] in the endowments of the head" (Kramnick 663-67). Thus, keeping blacks in bondage failed to make him feel out of joint with his belief that "all men are created" with a right to "life, liberty, and the pursuit of happiness."

Benjamin Banneker, the black mathematician, who had a hand in the design of the nation's capital in the District of Columbia and published a popular almanac in the country during the 1790s, tried to detach Jefferson from

---

6. See Jordan, 464-69. DNA tests recently confirmed the relationship.

the Blackwall Hitch. Banneker fully understood that white Americans, save some exceptions, were hooked on a habit of pairing whiteness with brains and blackness with brawn. He wrote a letter to Jefferson while the latter was serving as secretary of state. In it, Banneker laments that there is an "almost general prejudice" in the country "against those of my complexion" (Porter 1971, 324). The view, he cries, casts "an eye of contempt" on blacks and has them falsely seem "rather as brutish than human, and scarcely capable of mental endowments." Banneker says that what usually "prevails with respect to [blacks]" is a "train of absurd and false ideas and opinions." Proud that he is a black of "the deepest dye," he observes "that one universal Father" has truly "afforded us all the same sensations and endowed us all with the same faculties," no matter "however diversified in situation or color" (325). He indicates that black people suffer "many difficulties and disadvantages" due to the current bias against them; for their relief, he recommends that Jefferson and his fellow whites "wean [themselves] from those narrow prejudices which [they] have imbibed" about his "brethren" (326-27).

Equiano presents a similar case in his book. He tries "to remove the prejudice that some conceive" against Africans "on account of their color." In his opinion, the world's Creator did not "forebore to stamp understanding" on humans ebony in hue. Any "apparent inferiority" of blacks enslaved by whites might "naturally be ascribed to their situation" (45). He continues:

> When [Africans] come among Europeans, they are ignorant of their language, religion, manners, and customs. Are pains taken to teach them these? Are they treated as men? Does not slavery itself depress the mind, and extinguish all its fire and every noble sentiment? But, above all, what advantages do not a refined people possess, over those who are rude and uncultivated? (45-46)

He finishes with the wish that "such reflections as these [will dissolve white chauvinism] into sympathy for the [hardships] of their sable brethren, and compel them to acknowledge that understanding is not confined to feature or color" (46).

Equiano in unison with Banneker would have had an easy time picking up the sympathy of John Woolman. But then, the Quaker broke from the Blackwall Hitch long before either black man issued a public remark. In 1762, Woolman contended that social conditions had degraded people of African descent and fixed "a notion in the mind" of whites about blacks as "a sort of people below [them] in nature" (Kramnick 631). He urged his fellows to accept that black "understandings and morals are equal" to that of white men in general (634). The Quaker warned whites that their bias against blacks functioned as the source of "a great enemy to true harmony in [the] country." He said that there really "is nothing in it sufficient to induce a wise man to choose it" (636).

Neither Equiano nor Banneker, though, could have moved Jefferson to side with Woolman. Like eighteenth-century whites in general, the third president died with his unflattering view of blacks intact. He responded to the letter from Banneker with the suggestion that the black man actually counted as an aberration. "Nobody wishes more than I do," Jefferson answered, "to see such proofs as you exhibit, that nature has given to our black brethren talents equal to those of the other colors of men; and that the appearance of the want of them is owing merely to the degraded condition" of their lives (Porter 328). In other words, Jefferson seriously doubted that Banneker with his intelligence typified the average black. In the white's eyes, most blacks remained short on smarts and slated for slavery throughout their lives.

If Jefferson and his peers, riveted to the Blackwall Hitch, had dispassionately looked to see how the *African* and the *Autobiography* measure up to one another, they would have halted without room to wonder whether or not bright blacks like Banneker and Equiano were either common or curious among their fellows. A comparison of the manner in which Equiano and Franklin handle swimming in their autobiographies guarantees that blacks in their day failed to match whites in stature, not for want of reason but because of suffering from undue oppression fostered by a specious impression. In the *Autobiography*, Franklin says that he learned to swim well early; he illustrates that he was able to master the feat thanks to having a place to swim, given his boyhood home near the water in Boston, in addition to having the persistence to study and practice the maneuver. During his first stay in London, he perceives himself able to "open a Swimming School," from which, if he dared to, he could earn "a good deal of Money" ([1791] 1993, 65). Swimming never strikes Equiano in the same way. Raised until eleven, in a valley beyond the site of "any water larger than a pond or a rivulet" (Equiano [1798] 1995, 53), the black regrets having missed an opportunity to learn how to swim at home. Since, on the ships, where his youth is spent in slavery, white mates guard against his escape by barring him from mastering the trick to staying afloat, Equiano does not know how to keep himself up in deep water, and as a result, in the swim of things during his days at sea, his fortunes hang in the balance; in fact, on a few occasions, swift assistance from a kind swimmer just saves him from drowning. Side by side, the books from Equiano and Franklin symbolize how American society was obliging to whites, yet adverse to blacks; they picture how black people, due to the Blackwall Hitch, faced shallow opportunities to acquire and apply skills with which to earn a decent living, while whites lucked upon a flood of channels open to profitable pursuits.

The ironic black accent invoked by the given state of affairs surfaces conspicuously in Equiano's story when he recalls how he piloted a ship at risk and steered it safely into port. The event takes place after Equiano has paid his master forty pounds sterling, from his private side-business revenue, in order to gain his freedom. Bearing the title "freeman" (120), he has volunteered for this voyage, circling from Montserrat to Savannah. He meets trouble in Georgia. "A slave belonging to Mr. Read, a merchant of Savannah," tests "all the patience" of which Equiano is master, by striking him and forcing Equiano to fall on him "and beat him soundly." In the morning, the slave's owner demands to have Equiano "flogged all round the town, for beating his Negro slave," which, in legal terms, amounts to damaging his private property. Equiano feels squeezed into a tight corner; "I knew," he says, "there was little or no law for a Negro free here" (121); he figures that he could never get a fair trial by jury in the district and he guesses that he would be lucky to experience no more than a whipping from Mr. Read and his fellow townsmen. In Savannah, he recalls, a free black carpenter was jailed and later expelled from the area "for asking the gentleman that he worked for, for the money he had earned" (122).

After some fear and trembling, Equiano senses "a rage" seizing his "soul," which provokes in him a resolve "to resist the first man that should offer to lay violent hands" on him; he thinks, "I would sooner die like a free man, than suffer myself to be scourged by the hands of ruffians, and my blood drawn like a slave" (122), and he probably would have died fighting for liberty, without a hand from Captain Thomas Farmer, who has seen in Equiano a worthy sailor. Farmer entreats Read and his comrades to let the black man leave in peace, to which they consent, after some delay, and Equiano is very thankful, but the mishap has slowed the ship's activity, and it provokes the captain to regard him as an undue burden. Going on, Equiano implies that waves of bigotry have fueled a climate in which people of color are apt to look like social problems, and yet sadly the perspective places white and black lives in jeopardy. He relates how the captain and first mate fall sick during the return passage; full responsibility for the vessel, its crew, and cargo lands on Equiano's shoulders; the action shifts into a rather hazardous journey as the sea turns rough and swamps the ship with a deluge that impels the crew to man "the pumps every half or three quarters of an hour" (124). The problem is worsened by the reality that whites, in spite of his expressed desire to learn, have denied Equiano a fair chance to study navigation, for they have viewed a black man unfit to acquire such knowledge. Equiano wryly relates, "The captain was now very sorry he had not taught me navigation." Nevertheless, the black man takes charge and proves to be the [agent] of the ship's deliverance out of harm's way; "by the mere dint of reason" (124), he directs the vessel out of danger. "Many were surprised," he says, "when they heard of [his] conducting the sloop into port, and [he] obtained a new [name], and was called Captain" (125); through the episode, Equiano implies that equal justice works in the interest of everyone.

Throughout his work, he invites his audience to see that blacks have what it takes to pass muster in America; they have minds that loaded with useful knowledge, make it possible for them to captain their fates. His memoir bears the affect of a mistaken exception, proving the rule that "all men are created equal." Equiano offers himself as a sign to show that black people are not "incapable of learning." He composed his story knowing well, whites believed, black "minds are such barren soil or moor that culture would be lost on them; and that [blacks] come from a climate where nature, though prodigal of her [gifts] in a degree unknown to [whites], has left man alone scant and unfinished" (99-100). Equiano's life makes that kind of talk sound plainly "at once impious and absurd" (100).

If Franklin had read the *African* when it first appeared in print during the year before his death, the book's irony would hardly have been lost on him. The "founding father's" allegiance to the British Crown began to slacken in the 1760s; his view of blacks started to improve at the same time. Coming to see blacks capable of some learning in 1760 Franklin accepted a post that had him serve as a trustee for a foundation established to build a number of colonial charity schools, meant to convert enslaved blacks to Christianity. He visited one of the trial schools in 1763 and afterward reported to an acquaintance:

> I was on the whole much pleas'd, and from what I then saw, have conceiv'd a higher Opinion of the natural Capacities of the black Race, than I had ever before entertained. Their Apprehension seems as quick, their Memory as strong, and their Docility in every Respect equal to that of white Children. You will won-

> der perhaps that I should ever doubt it, and I
> will not undertake to justify all my Prejudices,
> nor to account for them. (1987, 800)

The correspondence shows that Franklin's bias against blacks was slipping away. A year later, further proof appeared in his essay "Narrative of the Late Massacres, in Lancaster County, of a Number of Indians, Friends of this Province, by Persons Unknown," where he insinuates, some blacks have a stronger "Sense of Justice and Honor" than some whites "and that even the most brutal" black people seem more "capable of feeling the Force of Reason" (1987, 553) than some white folks.

In 1772, he published an editorial in the *London Chronicle*, airing enthusiasm about the Somerset Case, in which the presiding judge had decided that by landing in England a slave, named James Somerset, had become free, for slavery, ruled the judge, held no legal standing in the country; in his editorial, Franklin observes that it was just to set Somerset free, but liberating one black was nothing about which to brag as long as thousands more remained locked in chains; the author calls for a law to abolish "the African commerce in Slaves, and [to declare] the children of present Slaves free after they become of age" (1987, 677); he goes on to refer to the slave trade as a "detestable traffic in the bodies and souls of men" (678). In August, Franklin wrote to Anthony Benezet, a longtime abolitionist who had opened a school for blacks in Philadelphia two years before; with Benezet, he shared a hope that the land's practice of "keeping Negroes" would be "suppress'd by the Legislature" (876). By the 1780s, Franklin evinced a straightforward wish to see blacks receive equal treatment in the United States. In 1787, he became the Pennsylvania Abolitionist Society president and revitalized the coalition. From that office, he issued a public statement requesting an end to slavery, because it constituted "an atrocious debasement of human nature," accustoming a victim "to move like a mere machine" and thereby throttling thought, retarding choice, and bringing "reason and conscience" to submit to "the passion of fear" (1154-55). He

indeed had the fortunes of blacks in mind near the end of
his life when he published a resolution to furnish them with
"advice and instruction, protection from wrongs," plus
education and employment (1156); he as well wrote Gover-
nor John Langdon seeking to stop the practice of fitting
ships for the slave trade in Pennsylvania, which Franklin
found "so evidently repugnant to the [politics] and form of
government lately adopted by [the people in the nation] and
which cannot fail of delaying the [joy] of the blessing of
peace and liberty, by drawing down, the displeasure of the
great and impartial Ruler of the Universe upon our country" (1170). Three weeks before his death, as his final public deed, Franklin wrote "On the Slave Trade," satire critical of the new government's refusal to free blacks.

It is very noteworthy that six years prior to his death
Franklin surmised that blacks sustain the "Opinions of
the Americans." It happened just before he resumed writing his book (after a thirteen-year interval); he produced
an article to inform "many Persons in Europe" about the
merits of the land. He guesses that Americans were more
inclined to respect their fellows for having a skill and
using it well than for their lineage. "They are pleas'd," he
says, "with the Observation of a Negro, and frequently
mention it." Blacks would say, he relates:

> *Boccarorra* (meaning the Whiteman) make de
> black man workee, make de horse workee, make
> de Ox workee, make ebery ting workee; only de
> Hog. He, de hog, no workee; he eat, he drink,
> he walk about, he go to sleep when he please,
> *he libb like a Gentleman.* (1987, 975-77)

Franklin thereby attests that Americans despised any
man who considered himself born better than others and
hence worthy of their indulgence; mostly, they regarded
him as if he were a hog; they simply admired individuals
for the mixture, imagination and usefulness of all their
"Handiworks." Connotatively, Franklin finds that true
Americans call human dominion over others horrible; he
suggests that the land holds great promise, for the citizenry
perceives such a state as *"good for nothing"* (977), and none

of them has seen it better than blacks at the bottom of the social ladder.

The related documentation shows that if Franklin perused the *African* on the eve of his passing, he would have noticed, his personal narrative rests on the same grounds that lie beneath the black's book. Like his story, Franklin would have fathomed that Equiano's work colors "men" as beings born to profit from learning. Each text paints the talent as a pretext for freedom. Expressive of the creed animating the country, thus, epic in character, the hero in each instance stands closer to an artisan, if not an artist, than the warrior type in ancient legends. Then, too, the white man would have been ready to acknowledge that a tonal shift sets his manuscript apart from Equiano's text. Franklin could have figured that the two books speak with different accents. He would have determined that an unsound score of black worth composed the critical source of the separation.

Neither book was in press in October 1785, when both men resided in Philadelphia. But, by that month, their sights were equally set well beyond the scope of their elders' horizons. They then disdained rigid hierarchies. A fluid democracy had come to represent an ideal state in their minds. So, if they had bumped into one another on a Philadelphia street, they could have enjoyed a good talk. Equiano could have informed Franklin of his recent visit to the Benezet school for blacks, which pleased him, for it was a place, he felt, where black "minds are cultivated" in order to turn the individual owners into "useful members of the community" (Equiano [1789] 1995, 186). Indeed, the sentiment would have secured Franklin's goodwill.

3

Crow's Nest

Education means to inspire people to live more abundantly, to learn to begin with life as they find it and make it better.
— *The Mis-education of the Negro*, Carter G. Woodson

In August 1834, a Boston youth, looking to rest his weary eyes cast aside his Harvard education and went to sea on a ship named the *Pilgrim*, bound for the remote California coast via Cape Horn. That same month, a less fortunate fellow stranded near the shores of Baltimore fought to press his slaveholder from treating him as a beast of burden. While the two Americans embarked on polar paths, they landed in bordering fields under a decade later when one produced a book and the other presented a lecture in the state of Massachusetts. Matching vistas surfaced in their converse travels and moored their sights at parallel points. From distinct angles, they came to confirm a paradigm of "men" instrumental to the formulation of the United States of America.

    The first youth was Richard Henry Dana, Jr. A European American from Boston Brahmins, he authored the memoir *Two Years before the Mast* (1840), recounting his trials as a common sailor. Frederick Douglass was the second young man. Born an American slave, probably from an out of wedlock affair between his black mother and a white man,[1] Douglass ran from bondage, by land as well as by sea, two warm Septembers after Dana had ended his voyage, and in 1841, prompted by William Lloyd Garrison, the black man began a speaking tour for the abolitionist movement; it was four years prior to the publication of his book, *Narrative of the Life of Frederick Douglass, an American Slave* (1845). His tale, with Dana's story, was widely read in antebellum society.

Popular opinions about the narratives have shifted from time to time. Great praise greeted their publications. The public deemed them attractive. But, neither remained nestled atop the best-seller list. Dana's lost its intrigue in the country sooner than Douglass's did. Though *Before the Mast* was a hit, recognizable as one of its time's "most successful American books," Harper & Brothers, which published it, mishandled it. In the months before 1868, when the initial copyright expired, few were stocked in stores (Adams 1890, 26). Like similar personal histories penned by slaves, comparable to those written by blacks such as Moses Roper, William Wells Brown, and Josiah Henson,[2] *An American Slave*[3] outsold prose works from Henry David Thoreau and Nathaniel Hawthorne, in addition to Herman Melville, and the slave narrative drew greater notice as the Civil War approached; in fact, around the middle of the 1800s, the period said by F. O. Matthiessen to represent "the American Renaissance," only fiction from women (Susan Warner, if not, Fanny Fern surpassed in appeal slave narratives akin to Douglass's achievement.[4]

---

1. In his edition of Douglass's *Narrative in the Life of Frederick Douglass, an American Slave* (1993), David Blight speculates in footnote #3 that Douglass's three personal histories taken together leave his father's identity mysterious, but recent scholarship suggests that Douglass's father was either a European American slave-overseer named Aaron Anthony or one who was a slaveowner named Thomas Auld. For further information, see Dickson J. Preston, *Young Frederick Douglass* (1980) and William McFeely, *Frederick Douglass* (1991).

2. Henson inspired Harriet Beecher Stowe to write her novel *Uncle Tom's Cabin* (1852).

3. Henceforth, I refer to Douglass's work as *An American Slave* and Dana's as *Before the Mast* for I believe that the abbreviated titles are most apt.

4. See Frances S. Foster's *Witnessing Slavery* (Wisconsin, 1979), pages 22-23.

Before the Mast has since attracted faint scholarly interest. In 1847, the Massachusetts board of education secretary, Horace Mann, aspired to adopt the publication for use in the school system; in his diary, Mann beckoned Dana to revise his work for educational purposes; the Secretary said, "the book fell off in interest at the close, that the final chapter was wanting in the true, humane and [generous] spirit," probably due to haste, and that the text should feature more utilitarian facts, yet, through sound revisions, the material "could be pressed into the service of education." The educator never realized the wish, first of all, because Harper & Brothers controlled the copyright for the story, but, second, because Mann's criticism infuriated Dana and prompted him to judge the educator preposterous (Adams 1890, 118-120). A long lull passed, until another scholar commented on Dana's memoir *Before the Mast*. Americans in academics virtually ignored it up to the 1930s. Actually, to date, the book has generated hardly a dozen studies in journals. "The Composition, Reception, Reputation, and Influence of *Two Years before the Mast*," an unpublished doctoral dissertation, written by Robert Francis Lucid at the University of Chicago in 1958, perhaps holds the most rigorous examination of the text. Other inquiries typically have dwelled on factual errors in the report or its standing as a maiden voyage into American literary Realism.

A critical 1989 publication, *Recovering Literature's Lost Ground* strives to keep Dana's memoir from "slipping from academic consciousness." In a chapter on *Before the Mast*, the solemn author James Cox rues that "the leading American literature anthologies now run toward [about] five thousand pages, but not a page is Dana's" (55). The critic finds that a main cause for which Dana's book receives perfunctory treatment, at best, is linked to his having "come to be associated with the genteel tradition" of old New England that has fallen out of favor. "But there is a second and much more important reason for [it]: the rediscovery of Herman Melville" (56), who, after reading and admiring Dana's work, created *Moby Dick* (1851) and so rendered it difficult to admire (57) the former work. It will be terribly lamentable, Cox says, if *Before the Mast* fades into oblivion, for it represents "a profound expression of the culture" (58).

Grasping Dana's saga as an iconic national form, D. H. Lawrence saved it from obscurity in 1923, when he published his *Studies in Classic American Literature*, with sarcastic remarks about Dana's narrative, subsequent to a mocking of Benjamin Franklin, prior to some scoffing at Melville. Lawrence guessed that a native spirit animates every land. It was true in the case of American society as far as the English novelist could see. In his *Studies*, he emphatically states:

> Every continent has its own great spirit of place. Every people is polarized in some particular locality, which is home. . . . Different places on the face of the earth have different vital effluence, different vibration, different chemical exhalation, different polarity with different stars: call it what you like. But the spirit of place is a great reality. The Nile valley produced not only the corn, but the terrific religions of Egypt. ([1923] 1964, 6-7)

Inadvertently, echoing St. John de Crevecoeur, as well as Frederick Jackson Turner, who regarded to the country as a novel society shaped by a peculiar environment, Lawrence speaks of it as a place that turns inhabitants into a rare breed. He says, "China produces the Chinese, and will go on doing so. The Chinese in San Francisco will in time cease to be Chinese, for America is a great melting-pot" (7). According to Lawrence, a contagious climate has borne an odd human strain content to cultivate a barbarous literary harvest unsavory to the Old World palate. Classic American literature stakes, he claims, that folks in the land mean to be "masterless" (5), to reject every form of external authority as an unnatural imposition.

Lawrence offers Dana's disgust at the sight of floggings on the *Pilgrim*, by order of the captain, as an authentic sign of the spirit that moves Americans. The novelist thinks that Sam the "fat slow fellow" on board, who galls the captain, merits a whipping for disturbing the standard "reciprocity of command and obedience" (116). Lawrence never fancies freedom and democracy yielding a principled society or a prosperous ship; he takes it for granted that a rigid hierarchy is imperative for success in either case. It is a fact, he fathoms, that Americans are too idealistic to accept. Hence, they fail to treasure keeping master-and-servant bonds intact. A commitment to equality is farcical, for it defies nature where polarity reigns, maintains Lawrence. Dana's reply to the flogging proves how romantic Americans are. The scene reminds the Englishman of the intense interval in Melville's *White-Jacket* (1850) in which the protagonist "was once going to be flogged" ([1923] 1964, 119). With Melville standing for the American hero, beginning at least with Franklin, Lawrence says, Melville "would have taken [the beating] as the last insult" (119).

Cox defends Lawrence's premise that Americans would prefer not to take any indignity. He states that "the dramatic high point" in *Before the Mast* comes when two in Dana's crew suffer a flogging by order of their captain (Cox 1989, 59). Cox discovers in the event proof that an urge to reform standard relations "between ship captains and crew—or, we might say, between masters and men" (58) launched Dana's book and gave it an "expression of and relation to the cultural . . . issues of nineteenth-century America" (60). Thus, while the critic disagrees with how Lawrence chides the culture, he grades the Englishman's estimate "very helpful" (61) in a whirl to get a fix on the air streaming through *Before the Mast*. Cox has it emanating from the main currents of the national wellspring.

Reviewers have seen Douglass's slave narrative similarly. Their verdicts have pictured the book as very American in design. They have conveyed the idea that an epic quality circulates in the text. In fact, their ideas foster a mood to swallow that *An American Slave* and *Before the Mast* rest on a common foundation. Then too, others have charged Douglass's manuscript with issuing from a social orientation estranged from select white discourse. Such notions have clouded agreement in the writings of blacks and whites. The last point of view has held sway in recent years among analysts of African American arts.

Since black studies programs fast arose, late in the 1960s, an initiative to place black expressions apart from white ones has ruled research in the field. Attuned to the separatist politics of the Black Power movement, the given approach has washed over glimmers of unanimity among citizens who differ in color. Rather than highlight connections, it has spotlighted divisions. Addison Gayle pioneered the critical development through the publication of *The Black Aesthetic* (1971), an anthology which he edited and dedicated to deriving a pertinent scale for weighing beauty in black writings. Houston A. Baker, trailing Gayle, in 1972, released his *Long Black Song*, juxtaposing black and white utterances to inscribe them within the cultural matrix as unambiguous contradictions. Henry Louis Gates advanced the approach the furthest. In his acclaimed publication *The Signifying Monkey* (1988), he portrays black writing as a talent imported from Africa and implemented in America as a measure of mutiny against the mainstream.

Springing from the mandated wave of criticism, Stephen Butterfield in *Black Autobiography in America* (1974) situates Douglass's work in an autobiographical tradition where "Black writers offer a model of the self which is different from white models," forged in reaction to white historical visions and betraying atypical, generally contradictory "meanings to human actions" (2). Butterfield also argues that "the concept of identity" present in most celebrated "white personal narratives since the [American] Renaissance, is the individual forging" a route to success through the exploitation of others, whereas "the 'self' of black autobiography," principally, reflecting a bad landing among whites suffered by blacks, "is not an individual" with a personal agenda, "but a soldier in a long, historic march" to a promised land of communal bliss (2-3). Baker echoes this understanding in his essay "Autobiographical Acts and the Voice of the Southern Slave." Prior to calibrating *An American Slave*, he imparts that white memoirs air an idea of a heroic figure

as a man on his own, in search of "self-definition and salvation," with divine approval, and the image starkly con-
flicts with the model pursuit in black American autobiography. Baker calls Douglass's book "one of the finest black
American slave narratives," serving "to illustrate the
black autobiographer's" peerless struggle for personal success (Andrews 1991, 95-96). Furthermore, in "Narration,
Authentication, and Authorial Control in Frederick Douglass's *Narrative* of 1845" and "Frederick Douglass's 1845
Narrative," Robert B. Stepto and Robert O'Meally, respectively, supply pretexts to isolate the African American
autobiography from life stories by white Americans. Gates
captures the current coterie's drift in "Binary Oppositions
in Chapter One of *Narrative of the Life of Frederick Douglass an American Slave Written by Himself*" where he
determines Douglass's work to be typical of "an ordering
of the world based on a profoundly relational type of
thinking," hemmed within "a strict barrier of difference,"
in lieu of likenesses (Andrews 1991, 86). He theorizes that
the ideation of *An American Slave* is receptive to being
rated "the first charting of the black hermeneutical circle"
(91).

The black art theories submerged an older tide, per
se, flowing out of the Civil Rights movement, dating back
to the country's victory in World War II, and declaring
that black mores feed and savor the mainstream. Scholars
like Arna Bontemps, J. Saunders Redding, and Benjamin
Quarles sustained this point of view. Margaret Just Butcher's *The Negro in American Culture* (1956), divulges the
alliance's stance. Butcher avows:

> The right and most effective way to look at the
> Negro's relationship to American culture is to
> consider it not as an isolated race matter and
> minority group concern, but rather in the con-
> text of the whole of American culture. [At
> once] one inevitably——and rightly——becomes
> involved with the history and fortunes of both
> the majority and the minority groups. These
> fortunes are not separate; nor can they be
> separately evaluated or understood. They
> overlap and interlock. . . . Together, and only

> together, they have interwoven the vital,
> sturdy patterns of American society. (Butcher
> [1956] 1972, 3)

Kenny J. Williams amplifies the philosophy in *They Also Spoke*, her 1970 "attempt to re-tell the story of [African American] literature in America through a focus on some of the dominant motifs of our national literature." She muses:

> After all, Negro literature is really American
> literature —nothing more nor nothing less. . . .
> To continue to look at Negro literature as a
> separate phenomenon is to miss the totality of
> American literature itself, a literature which
> necessarily is a result of the multitude of
> national and racial strains which constitute
> the nation. (xi)

Rebecca Chalmers Barton drafted the older critics' blueprint for looking at black letters. Disseminating the method in *Witnesses for Freedom* (1948), Barton postulates that *An American Slave*, with other African American memoirs, harbors an intelligible character that has earned it "an integral place in American letters" (274). Bolstering her remark about the genre, she says, "The Negro Americans who come to life in these pages display the same variety of taste, temperament, and purpose as any other segment" of American society (282). She never had a quarrel with Butcher, whose own digging extracts from Douglass's narrative "a dramatic universal appeal" and reveals, "As time goes on, the career and character of [Douglass] take on [ever more] the stature and significance of the epical" (145). Concurring with Barton, Bontemps extends Butcher's observation that a legendary property surrounds Douglass's personal history. Discussing slave narratives in general and *An American Slave* in particular, he sees that Douglass's work is the most engaging form of a literary style crafted by African Americans and providing their "worthiest contribution to American literature" (1969, xiv); moreover, he indicates, the manuscript "was felt by many readers of the nineteenth century to epitomize the condition of man on the earth as it documented the personal history of the individual to whom bondage was real and freedom was more than a dream" (vii); the narrative became "a parable" whose "theme was the fetters of mankind and the yearning of all living things for freedom" (xviii).

The readers who have credited an epic magnitude to the book have not materialized without a precursor. In a review from 1849, Ephraim Peabody likens it to Homeric myths. He positions Douglass's work "among the most remarkable productions of the age," since they picture slavery, display "under a new light the mixed elements" of the land, and offer "a vivid exhibition of the force and working of the native love of freedom in the individual mind." Following an equation of the text with the *Iliad*, Peabody says, "Or if the Iliad should be thought not to present a parallel case, we know not where one who wished to write an [up-to-date] Odyssey could find a better subject than in the adventures" of a freedman (Andrews 1991, 24), like Douglass. Peabody's old review welcomes hailing *An American Slave* for embodying an epic thrust.

If Lawrence was correct, and a preference against suffering any indignity characterizes a national classic, Douglass's book shares that trait in common with *Before the Mast*. As Cox has testified, "the dramatic high point in Dana's narrative" occurs around the brutal flogging scene. During that moment, it climaxes. The deal is the same in Douglass's story. The account peaks once the hero resists being beaten. Paired, *An American Slave* and Dana's book validate claims that invite reading the black man's work as a national invention.

A motif advocating that society should authorize its citizens to conduct lives by their own initiative, rather than acquiesce to the authority of others, wends its way through the episodes in Dana's recollection of his passages at sea. The theme dispatches the tale's major tack. It rigs the story to treasure democracy. Its bearing volunteers slavery as a barbarism. It gears the text to hail equal justice for all who in his eyes are "men."

Before the Mast starts with the protagonist wishing to step easily into what he expects to be a romantic pursuit, being a sailor on a merchant ship; he imagines that the job will invigorate him. He notices, though, as he heaves his first sail, that he stands apart "from the regular *salt*" whose hands are "bronzed and toughened" from hours of labor in the sun (Dana [1840] 1986, 41); still, Dana plans to fit in. The initial results embarrass him. He screws up his chores and suffers seasickness, too. Luckily, he meets sympathy among his fellow mates. The cook, an older black man, is especially kind to him. In just two weeks, they help him to adapt, to get his "sea legs on" (48). A little over a month later, once the ship has crossed the equator, he is seasoned enough to go on watch in the crow's nest and "to keep a bright look-out" (60).

His buoyant outlook lasts a brief spell. On the first day at sea, a speech from the captain foreshadows trouble ahead. Capt. Thompson informs every member of his crew:

> Now, my men, we have begun a long voyage. If we get along well together, we shall have a comfortable time; if we don't, we shall have hell afloat.—All you've got to do is obey your orders and do your duty like men,—then you'll fare well enough;—if you don't, you'll fare hard enough, —I can tell you. (43)

The address settles the conduct code, on board; it outlaws liberty and equality, as it decrees total submission to the captain, who "is lord paramount . . . and must be obeyed" without the slightest hesitation (50). Dana soon perceives that the policy supports a pyramidal hierarchy, licensing an awful tyranny.

The despotism sanctioned by the *Pilgrim*'s chain of command begins to hit Dana fully when the captain demotes Foster, the second mate, to an ordinary seaman and presents the officer's post to another sailor. That incident alerts Dana to the captain's weight. He gathers that it favors the authority of a slavemaster, who handles human beings like brutes in his custody. The flogging scene shows how the system on the merchant ship authorized the commander of the crew to bully his charges. Witnessing the action disturbs Dana; he says, "A man— a human being, made in God's likeness —fastened up and flogged like a beast" (153). He is left disgusted and furious, yet too weak to object. An epiphany occurs as the captain orders Sam whipped for being lazy and sullen and inflicts the punishment on John the Swede for challenging his resolve to have Sam flogged; the captain cries:

> You see your condition! You see where I've got you all, and you know what to expect!—You've been mistaken in me—you didn't know what I was! Now you know what I am!—I'll make you toe the mark, every soul of you, or I'll flog you all, fore and aft, from the boy, up!—You've got a driver over you! Yes, *a slave-driver—a negro-driver!* I'll see who'll tell me he is n't a negro slave! (156)

His words impute that a common sailor is a match for a black slave; beyond exposing them to suns hot enough to turn their hands darker than black palms, conditions at sea for the regular salts have a tendency to color their lives a dusky hue evocative of black bondage.

Aptly, the story's crest succeeds the spotting of "a pilot-fish, the sure precursor of a shark," (93) next to the ship. In the rest of the tale, a long denouement unfolds through deft strokes. It confirms the impression made by the climax. Sailors are painted as individuals exploited as chattel. Their lives are short, nasty, and brutal, lived "under a tyranny," like a "poor class of beings" (157) not human. After twenty-two years in the business, one sailor feels "worked like a horse, and treated like a dog" (266). Heading for home on the *Alert*, while lying up sick several days in the dank forecastle, Dana himself identifies his situation as "the worst part of a dog's life" (399).

Effectively a slave, save his being "a gentleman's son" (350), Dana's voyage into bondage might have lasted far longer than two tough years; "the whole current of [his] future" could have taken a radical shift; he might have deviated into "a sailor for the rest of [his] days" (349). It is clear, as, "congratulating [himself] upon [his imminent] escape" from the hull of the *Pilgrim*, he gets a summons from Captain Thompson, which he answers just to learn that his "lord paramount" refuses to let him board a vessel, bound for Boston, unless he finds someone else to serve in his place aboard the *Pilgrim*, because the skipper assesses Dana as a vital bit of the ship's property, shy of a replacement. The captain assures Dana that he owns him and "that he [has] an absolute discretionary power" (349) in the situation. Shocked, Dana soon scurries in search of someone to substitute for him on the craft. Able to offer money and clothing in exchange for getting him off the hook, he manages to acquire a surrogate, "called Harry Bluff," a fellow "who [does] not care what country or ship he [is] in" and is glad to bid Dana "a pleasant passage home, jingling the money in his pocket" (351-52). The bargain sets Dana free from further brushes with the captain. It fails however to shield him from bitter recollections about the torture witnessed with his own eyes. He feels incensed whenever he recalls the "great cruelty inflicted upon [his] shipmates"; forever hence, merely "the simple mention of the word flogging," he plaintively testifies, "brings up in [him] feelings which [he] can hardly control" (469).

The same sort of rage surfaces in Douglass's book. His text denies humans the right to rule others by brute force; it calls for universal democracy. Vivid memories of inequality abound in it. They strike the black man as terrible wrongs. He hints that everyone merits useful knowledge and equal justice. In his view, such a state fosters good fortune. Tyranny and ignorance, on the other hand, whip people into animals in need of control.

Houston Baker and H. Bruce Franklin both have found that animal imagery spills from the pages *An American Slave*. For instance, in the opening paragraph, Douglass compares his life to being a horse in order to explain why he has to speculate about his birthday. "By far the larger part of the slaves know as little of their age as horses know of theirs," says the narrator, "and it is the wish of most masters within my knowledge to keep their

slaves thus ignorant." He recalls, "I do not remember to
have ever met a slave who could tell" his or her exact date
of birth (39). That confidence neatly sets the stage for a
parade of tropes sketching slavery as a system geared to
transform people into beasts.

During his boyhood on Colonel Lloyd's plantation,
too young to work in the fields, Douglass remembers, "The
most [he] had to do was to drive up the cows at evening, keep
fowls out of the garden," and otherwise aid "Master Daniel
Lloyd in finding his birds after he had shot them." His
responsibilities (shepherding, shooing, and spotting) suit
a dog. An occasional reward for his service, a nibble from
his master's "cakes" (53-54), would be right for a canine,
too. Douglass figures that his childhood represents a dog's
life at best. When he mentions his daily diet of mush dis-
pensed in "a large wooden tray or trough" for him and
other small children to eat with "oyster-shells" or "naked
hands," a reader sees that slavery forces its victims to live
"like so many little pigs" (54). Later, it is easy to realize
how a slave girl, such as Mrs. Hamilton's Mary, would be
disposed to fight with pigs for garbage (59).

"A den of wild beasts" (77) is a fitting description
for slavery. Douglass likens men and women in bondage
to animals. In addition, he attributes the same fate to the
masters of the system. Effectively, he paints the enslavers
and the enslaved as victims of the social institution. For
instance, among the whites, under its sway, Mrs. Sophia
Auld's "disposition [turns] to one of tiger-like fierceness"
(60). Mr. Thomas Auld, on the other hand, "might have
passed for a lion" (68). Plus, Mr. Edward Covey, a well-
seasoned slaveholder, exhibits the cunning of a snake.

Douglass's first slavemaster, known only as Capt.
Anthony, opens his eyes to the system's monstrous effect
through a "horrible exhibition," a "terrible spectacle." The
grizzly scene, the horror, the nightmare, enacted under the
cover of darkness in his white slavemaster's big house,
starkly foreshadows "the blood-stained gate, the wretched
entrance to the hell of black slavery," into which the poor
black youth is swiftly dragged before he even has a chance
to resist the immense evil. His innocent young eyes wit-

ness with distress an outrageous incident in which Capt.
Anthony in a mad outburst of sexual jealousy takes to giving a very ugly beating to his Aunt Hester,[5] "a woman of
noble form, and graceful proportions," with scarcely any
peers, "and fewer superiors, in personal appearance,
among colored or white women." Capt. Anthony, well
"hardened by a long life of slaveholding," itches to whip
Douglass's relative for being "with a young man," who
had the audacity to court Hester when her master "desired
her presence." Capt. Anthony hauls Aunt Hester into his
kitchen, strips her naked from "neck to waist," (42) and
hangs her by the wrists on a meat hook. With heartless
strokes, he flogs her back until it bleeds; at the same time,
he yells, "Now, you d____d b___h, I'll learn you to diso-
bey my orders!" (43). The action substantiates Olaudah
Equiano's suspicion, related in his prior work, that American slavery constituted a grim "new refinement in cruelty" (58) imposed on humanity.

For Douglass, a few savage murders amplify the
social order's true inhumanity. Mr. Austin Gore, "called
a first-rate overseer" (51), reckons that Demby has become
hopelessly "unmanageable" when the black slave plunges
"himself into a creek" and then refuses "to come out" for a
whipping; Mr. Gore gives the black man until the count of
three to come out or be shot. As Demby remains still in the
water after his time is up, the overseer raises his gun, fires
it, "and in an instant poor Demby [is] no more" (52). Mrs.
Giles Hicks later shows the same callous disregard for
black lives; she murders "a young girl" in her mid-teens,
by immediately "mangling her person in the most horrible manner, breaking her nose and breastbone with a
stick" for falling asleep at night in the midst of minding
the woman's baby and thus allowing the child's crying to
disturb the sleep of the mother. Furthermore, infuriated by
the sight of a hungry slave fishing on his own shoreline,
Mr. Beal Bondly quickly snatches his gun up and blows
"its deadly contents into the poor old man." The killers

---

5.   It is noteworthy that Douglass made "Aunt Hester" a household name before
Hawthorne wrote *The Scarlet Letter* (1850), starring Hester Prynne.

never pay a price for their homicides. Their "horrid" deeds uncover a savage mentality urging "little white boys" to think "that it was worth a half-cent to kill a 'nigger,' and a half-cent to bury one" (53).

Douglass provokes disgust for slavery's impact on him during his initial six months on Mr. Covey's farm. He is there for being "unsuitable to his [master's] purpose" (70). There is the insinuation that he has grown wild like a stubborn colt. Mr. Covey has acquired a reputation for taming unruly slaves. Hence, in consequence, Capt. Auld has resolved to lease Douglass to Mr. Covey for a year. Douglass cries, "I had been at my new home but one week before Mr. Covey gave me a very severe whipping, cutting my back causing the blood to run, and raising ridges on my flesh as large as my little finger" (71). "Scarce a week [passes] without his whipping [him]" (72) during the first half of the year.

He narrates being "made to drink the bitterest dregs of slavery" under Covey's rule. "Work, work, work was scarcely more the order of the day than of the night." It alters him. "I was somewhat unmanageable when I first went there, but a few months of this discipline tamed me." Approaching in manner a worn plow horse, likely to spend his leisure in a stupor under a tree, he says:

> Mr. Covey succeeded in breaking me. I was broken in body, soul, and spirit. My natural elasticity was crushed, my intellect languished, the disposition to read departed, the cheerful spark that lingered about my eye died; the dark night of slavery closed in upon me; and behold a man transformed into a brute! (74)

For his own humanity, Douglass revolts. The deed connotes a bridge to cross from a beastly life. The reported state of affairs leaves one ready to cheer the moment that the black slave resists Mr. Covey's effort to whip him in the stable, the hot day,[6] when he is sick of being used "like a

---

6. Douglass in his narrative writes that he fought Covey in 1833. But he was wrong about the date. It occurred in August 1834. For more details, see Preston (1980).

brute" (79). Soon tripped to the floor by the slavebreaker,
Douglass "resolve[s] to fight" and in accord "seize[s] Covey
hard by the throat," and as he does so, he proceeds to rise
(78), literally and figuratively as well. He wrestles with
the white slaveholder "for nearly two hours," until Covey,
"puffing and blowing at a great rate," quits and thereafter
never dares to try beating Douglass again. The episode
symbolizes effectively "a glorious resurrection from the
tomb of slavery to the heaven of freedom." Reviving
within Douglass "a sense" of his own humanity, the "battle
with Mr. Covey [is] the turning-point in [his] career as a
slave" (79).

Douglass echoes Dana's opinion. In material, he
confers a narrative that assumes a noble cast in the local
cultural context. His book corresponds to an epistle from a
civil religion, authorizing people to chart their own course.
It categorizes slavery with barbaric conduct and explains
"men" as creatures with a mind for liberty. It symbolized
a model discursive construction in the middle of the nineteenth century, reflecting the crystallization of a faith,
centering on the worship of "self-made men." A cultural
study of the narrative in relation to the intellectual currents covering the age renders this rather apparent.

Between 1820 and 1860, the time during which the
story at issue was born to applause, a sea of quests for integrity bolstered by instruction swept over the land from the
shore to the frontier. It was a Romantic upsurge of the sentiments that charged the American Revolution. Toting a
broad charm, the consciousness started to soar in January
1821, when Benjamin Lundy issued his paper the "Genius
of Universal Emancipation," hailing universal suffrage.
It peaked midway through the years in question. Overall,
under its sway, campaigns to expand females rights, end
black slavery, and erect public schools ran rampant. The
domestic mood plunged the nation into the Civil War, with
the eventual victors feeling immersed in a holy crusade.

By the 1820s, women were rather ready set to start a
revolution of their own, for they recognized themselves as
snubbed citizens denied their civil rights. Current laws
defined them as the private property of men without the

right to own any property or the privilege to vote for any leaders. Dynamic individuals such as Lucretia Mott and Elizabeth Cady Stanton protested that the circumstance was out of line with the social ethos decreed in the Declaration of Independence. Proclaiming themselves rational beings with a birthright to live by their own designs, the women looked for ways to capsize the passing patriarchy. They validated Abigail Adams's prophecy to her husband that "if particular care and attention is not paid to the ladies," they are surely going "to foment a rebellion, and will not hold [themselves] bound by any laws in which [they] have no voice or representation" (Schneir 1972, 3). John Adams received his spouse's warning in 1776, a few months before Jefferson drafted his revolutionary tract; while the woman's statement went unnoticed by most males in the country, the resolve that it broadcast was strong enough in 1848 to spark the first woman's rights gathering, held at Seneca Falls, where the scores of female participants in attendance adopted the Declaration of Sentiments and Resolutions, stating:

> We hold these truths to be self-evident: that all men and women are created equal. . . . The history of mankind is a history of repeated injuries and usurpations on part of man toward woman, having in direct object the establishment of an absolute tyranny over her. . . . He has monopolized nearly all the profitable employment, and from those she is permitted to follow, she [gets] but a scanty remuneration. He has denied her the facilities for obtaining a thorough education, all colleges being closed against her. . . . He has endeavored, in every way that he could, to destroy her confidence in her own powers, to lessen her self-respect, and to make her willing to lead a dependent and abject life. . . . Now, in view of the entire disfranchisement of one half the people of this country, their social and religious degradation . . . and because women do feel themselves aggrieved, oppressed, and fraudulently deprived of their most sacred rights, we insist that they have

immediate admission to the rights and privileges which belong to them as citizens of the
United States. (Schneir 77-80)

The document proves that the women were sure that Jefferson should have used "humans" in place of "men" when he
wrote his work. It guarantees that the women deemed
every one of them born to live free of others and believed
that they could benefit themselves quite well with learning
and liberty.

The women's convention resulted from an 1840
meeting between Mott and Stanton abroad in England at
an anti-slavery conference. It was fitting. Freeing blacks
and educating them had long attracted the early femi-
nists. In slavery, they spotted a symbol for a state in viola-
tion of national principles. The women deduced that men
were forcing them to suffer a form of the offense. In her
Woman in the Nineteenth Century (1845), Margaret
Fuller captures the women's perspective, as she speculates
that "there exists in the minds of men a tone of feeling
toward women as toward slaves" (Schneir 65).

Abolitionism, the movement to end black slavery,
served as the source for much social agitation; it struck a
great many as the ultimate test of the nation's mettle. To
the uninformed, the initiative "seemed suddenly to burst
upon the public in the 1830s, but this was only because a new
and more radical ingredient had been added" to the development (Filler 1960, 26). Talk against slavery ebbed and
flowed over the land from the earliest moments of the
land's gestation.[7] In 1688, on a Philadelphia hill, devout
Quakers drafted the first official protest "against 'the traffic of men-body'" (Quarles 1987, 43). Subsequently, a year
never passed without a flurry of struggles to liberate and
school blacks, initiated by individuals such as William
Penn, John Woolman, and Anthony Benezet. Early in the
eighteenth century, Samuel Sewall printed in Boston *The
Selling of Joseph*, cursing black slavery, in the process of
granting human beings, regardless of their skin color, a

---

7. For an excellent discussion of abolitionist literature, see Turner (1929).

natural right to chart their own course in life. Likewise, in the 1780s, Franklin penned criticism of the institution; actually, in 1729, for a Quaker, named Ralph Sandiford, Franklin issued through his press an attack on bondage entitled *A Brief Examination of the Practice of the Times*. Still, before William Lloyd Garrison came on the scene, the rhetoric tended to sound sanguine.

Garrison fired up the debate with the first edition of his radical paper the *Liberator*, demanding a quick end to slavery everywhere in the country. The hour had been set for such urgency. Garrison's predecessors had expressed their opinions in more hopeful tones for they had assumed that slavery stood as a "peculiar institution" which could not last because aware citizens were bound to root it out with all deliberate speed. Jefferson had shared the feeling with George Washington; aptly, each man freed his slaves after his death. Neither ever imagined that Eli Whitney would invent the cotton gin in 1793 and turn plantation slavery into a virtual gold mine. With the early phases of the Industrial Revolution then erupting, a huge wholesale global market for cotton formed and excited a steady interest in putting blacks to use as cheap labor in the trade; under the circumstances, the 1820 Missouri Compromise, permitting slavery to stretch into fresh territory, drove abolitionists to worry that the rotten business was going to infest unsettled parts of the country and in a short season would ruin the entire culture. In 1831, nine months after the *Liberator* was born, the bloody revolt in Virginia led by Nat Turner presented itself to abolitionists as a sign that the nation was headed for doom unless it abolished black slavery with deliberate speed.

Galvanized by Garrison, abolitionism flooded the land from the North to the South during the three decades before the Civil War; in its wake, it absorbed a majority of the era's most noted men of letters. For example, the poet John Greenleaf Whittier wrote verses, like the "Hunters of Men" (1834), against slavery. While Congressmen went muzzled by an 1836 gag order, silencing abolitionist cries in their hall, Thoreau fretted that his money would be used to fund a victory in the Mexican War and free Texas to invest in black slavery; the situation incited him to spend a long night in prison for refusing to pay his taxes, and it inspired him to write "Resistance to Civil Government" (1849). After the 1850 Fugitive Slave Law was put into effect, ruling it a federal offense to harbor a runaway slave, Emerson often gave addresses like "Address to the Citizens of Concord" (1851), denouncing the keeping of blacks in bondage. In *Mardi* (1849), Melville, counting bondage an abomination, foresees eternal damnation for masters, who steal babies from their mothers' breasts or wives from their husbands' arms to sell them for personal gain; on top of that, after having Ishmael wonder in *Moby Dick*, "Who aint a slave?" ([1851] 1964, 4), in his "Benito Cereno" (1855), he retells the story of an actual revolt aboard a real Spanish slaver and thereby insinuates that slavery threatens the social order. Dana the literary beacon who guided Melville to craft sea tales labored pro bono on behalf of slaves who had fled from their masters during the 1850s. Yet, the most influential of the local literati involved in the abolitionist movement was the woman named Harriet Beecher Stowe who authored Uncle *Tom's Cabin* (1852). Legend has it that Abraham Lincoln swore that her book alone ignited the Civil War.

The triumphant ethos granted "men" the privilege as well as the talent to prosper through the free use of knowledge. A push to build public schools unfolded. The sentiment propelled Philadelphia to establish a system of free grammar schools in 1836. By the 1850s, children all over the North had access to public schools. Mann, the Massachusetts education secretary, led this effort before engaging in national abolitionism. He captured the basic conviction of the social push for learning in 1848, when he reported to the state school board:

> Education . . . beyond all other devices of human origin, is the great equalizer of the conditions of men—the balance-wheel of the social machinery. [It] gives each man the independence and the means, by which he can resist the selfishness of other men. [If] this education should be universal and complete, it

would do more than all things else to obliter-
ate factitious distinctions in society (Ravitch
1990, 81).

To prove the usefulness of learning, he added, if a person
"will learn how to swim, he can fasten a dozen pounds'
weight to his back, and transport it across a narrow river"
(82). He leaves little grounds for doubting that the greatest
good is attainable by increasing human intelligence.

Transcendentalism, the epoch's most noted creed,
confirms the spread of a persistent vision, displaying the
heart of a religion throughout the length and breath of the
country; restating the Quaker belief that an "inner light"
is born in each and every human being waiting to shine,
the given cognizance advocated a spread of learning, too.
All people are endowed with a way to comprehend their surroundings through careful study and thus from birth have
the capacity to witness and stay on a fruitful path, the
Transcendentalists said. Learning to trust your own self
through intimacy with nature, they preached, swings open
the door to happiness. First among them, Emerson avowed
that all "men" form a bit of an "Oversoul," like an ocean
drop made to ebb and flow; sadly, societies everywhere,
since the dawn of civilization, have conspired to stifle the
human spirit by compelling "men" to abide by fixed forms;
yet, the best possible world promises to flower in America,
affording all a chance to thrive with the finesse of "a good
swimmer," whom "storms and waves can not drown"
(Emerson 1983, 709), once the country fully breaks the Old
World practice of requiring conformity, and liberally
schools the people to seek autonomy. "Whoso would be a
man," he claimed, "must be a nonconformist." Emerson
insisted, "Nothing can bring you peace but yourself" (261,
282). Hence, he evoked an effusion of knowledge with an
assurance that it would enable people to help themselves.

In the publication *Leaves of Grass* (1855), Walt
Whitman witnesses a rampant blossoming occurring in
the country. He imagines himself immersed in a magical
"wave of an hour" set to have a global ripple effect. The season, he forecasts, pages poets to produce "transcendant and

new" lyrics, implanting a passion for liberty, ripe "to cheer up slaves and horrify despots." As far as Whitman can tell "in the swimming shape" of the time, the nation grows daily into a zone of enterprise where lots of individuals work hard to turn over a new leaf and cultivate a novel existence, marking "the present spot the passage from what was to what shall be." Inadvertently, he grants Douglass his due in the land as he envisions, "A heroic person walks at his ease through and away from unsuitable social conditions (McMichael 1974, 1750-68). Also, in "Song of Myself," Whitman signifies that every segment of the culture draws on the same understanding:

> Or I guess it is a uniform hieroglyphic,
> And it means, Sprouting alike in broad zones and narrow zones,
> Growing among black folks as among white,
> Kanuck, Tuckahoe, Congressman, Cuff, I give them the same, I
> Receive them the same. (McMichael 1782-83)

The Good Gray Poet ends with a hint that a ubiquitous faith in open individualism thrives in the land nurtured by an equality of persons conditioned to unfold in the climate.

Whitman's reading was sound. By the time that he wrote, a consensus had in effect jelled; a secular religion had formed definitely. The many social movements were atmospheric products. It was conspicuous to Alexis de Tocqueville. The French aristocrat, touring the country, found in antebellum America an environment swarming with people loyal to shared social ideals. About the nation, Tocqueville observed:

> They hold that every man is born in possession of the right of self-government, and that no one has the right of constraining his fellow creatures to be happy. They have all a lively faith in the perfectibility of man, they judge that the diffusion of knowledge must necessarily be advantageous, and the consequences of ignorance fatal; they all [view] society as a body in a state of improvement, humanity as a changing scene, in which nothing is, or ought

> to be, permanent; and they admit that what
> appears to them today to be good, may be
> superseded by something better tomorrow.
> (Vol. 1, [1835] 1963, 393)

Moreover, regarding the fashion in which Americans
thought, he added:

> To evade the bondage of system and habit, of
> family maxims, class opinions, and, in some
> degree, of national prejudices; to accept tradi-
> tion only as a means of information, and exist-
> ing facts only as a lesson to be used in doing
> otherwise and doing better; to seek the reason
> of things for oneself, and in oneself alone; to
> tend to results without being bound to means,
> and to strike through the form to the sub-
> stance—such are the principal characteristics of
> what I shall call the philosophical method of
> Americans. [I]n most of the operations of the
> mind each American appeals [religiously] to the
> individual effort of his own understanding. . . .
> Everyone shuts himself up tightly within him-
> self and insists upon judging the world from
> there. (Vol. 2, [1840] 1963 3-4)

The Frenchman recognized that choice had become a matter of immense importance in American society; he saw
the flowering of the culture's values.

Within the climate, could a story about a savvy person who realizes autonomy fail to win acclaim? Tom Harris, the character in *Before the Mast* whom the narrator
calls "the most remarkable man I had ever seen" ([1840]
1986, 261), had to hit a responsive chord in the American
audience that welcomed him into the world. To the general
public, he had to seem like an ideal type, for he represents a
figure who has shed a poor, old life for a rich, new one by
developing his "reasoning powers" to a "remarkable"
degree. Harris keeps in his chest "several volumes" about
sailing and he readily reads them "with great pleasure."
Following years of study, he has become "a far better
sailor, and probably a better navigator, than the captain"
(264) and thereby secured for himself decent treatment.

Along with Franklin, Harris is a "self-taught" man who has risen in rank, through having "made himself master of" (263) some useful skills; yet, his triumph has not come with ease; he has had to overcome decades of drunkenness and "every sin that a sailor knows." Nevertheless, as his mind has matured, Harris has reached "the conviction that rum had been his worse enemy." So, "now a temperate man for life," he has become "capable of filling any berth in a ship" (266) and thus maintains an ability to find steady work.

The reception of George Ballmer had to clash with the keen manner in which Americans reacted to Harris. One symbolizes the antithesis of the other. Ballmer is "a lively, hearty fellow" (76), a festive guy who has neither mastered a skill nor achieved any resolve. He dies from a fall into the sea from a masthead with a load of tools strung around his neck. In a snap, he confronts "his death by drowning." After Ballmer's funeral, "many stories [are] told about George." They trust that his fate was fixed by his "never having learned to swim," added to the fact that, while he had changed his mind about making the voyage, he "was obliged to sail" against his will, for he had spent the sum of his advance and lacked the means to refund it (79). In the public eye, at first sight, Ballmer had to stand for a lost soul.

Ballmer and Harris illustrate that Dana grasped the sway of the social consciousness streaming across the country. He displays his keen awareness through his comparison of Sam's attitude and John the Swede's temper in the wake of their separate floggings. "John was a foreigner and high-tempered," says Dana, "and though mortified [actually] his chief feeling seemed to be anger." Sam, on the other hand, "was an American, and had had some education" and the whipping "coming upon him seemed to break him completely down. "He had a feeling of degradation that had been inflicted upon him, which the other man was incapable of." Sam ceased to share "queer negro stories" and "afterwards he seldom smiled, seemed to lose all life and elasticity, and appeared to have one wish, and that was for the voyage to be at an end" (184-85). Dana's moving reflection insinuates that despotism tries the American soul. It was a lesson that the author gleaned from his experience.

Douglass's reaction to tyranny marks him a man of native sensibilities. Oppression racked his mind. John the Swede's temper was foreign to Douglass. He felt debased more than disgraced by whippings. Douglass shared Sam's indigenous sense. In his mind, it was horrible for a "man" to suffer a beating from another human being.

Douglass came to see the land set on a mission to hold learning priceless, lives precious, liberty proper. An Appendix to *An American Slave* exhibits that the author grew to imagine the country running off course whenever it tolerated ignorance and bondage. First of all, the section cites "Clerical Oppressors," Whittier's abolitionist poem that finds hypocrisy in American slavery; a stanza cries:

> What! preach, and kidnap men?
> Give thanks, and rob thy own afflicted poor?
> Talk of thy glorious liberty, and then
> Bolt hard the captive's door? (Douglass 106)

Likewise, with a parody of a popular hymn, the Appendix paints devout slaveholders, like Covey, as social frauds. Rendered in verse, one bit remarks:

> They'll read and sing a sacred song,
> And make a prayer both loud and long,
> And teach the right and do the wrong,
> Hailing the brother, sister throng,
> With words of heavenly union. (108)

In addition, the supplement contains a biblical paraphrase that associates slaveholders in the country to monstrosities that favor "white sepulchres, which indeed appear beautiful outward, but are within full of dead men's bones, and of all uncleanness" (106).

Through his persona, Douglass upholds himself as an emblem in accord with local ideas. Symbolically, once Douglass escapes from slavery and arrives in New Bedford feeling "rescued by a friendly man-of-war from the pursuit of a pirate" (98), he must have shone in the eyes of his original audience. Around New Bedford, he watches laborers toil for their own benefit and discovers a rather fierce "determination to protect" (103) fugitives from capture; he depicts the setting as a Utopian site. "Every man appeared to understand his work," he says, "and went at it with a sober, yet [sunny sincerity], which betokened the deep interest which he felt in what he was doing, as well as a sense of his own dignity as a man" (102). The black has three practical lessons to thank for his triumph; their sources are Mrs. Auld, a textbook, and a newspaper.

Unwittingly, Mr. Auld hands him the best news that he ever hears; it occurs after the slaveholder stumbles upon his wife teaching Douglass how to spell words. The woman is rather new to slavery; "prior to her marriage," a weaver "by trade," she "had been dependent upon her own industry for a living." Before her husband intrudes, she exhibits a fond desire to educate Douglass, for she feels that it will serve him well; "her face," the narrator recalls, "was made of heavenly smiles, and her voice of tranquil music." By law her guardian, her husband alters her; Mr. Auld is an old hand at slavery; he turns Mrs. Auld hard and cold; he tells his wife that it is illegal and dangerous "to teach a slave to read" because "learning would *spoil* the best nigger in the world." Therefore, Mr. Auld insists, "A nigger should know nothing but to obey his master —to do as he is told to do" (57), and he commands Mrs. Auld to do as he tells her and never again try giving Douglass any schooling other than training in obedience. Anxious to oblige her husband, she follows his orders and commits herself to keeping the boy shut up "in mental darkness" as if he "were a brute" (59). Still, at the moment that Mr. Auld scolds his wife, Douglass learns "the pathway from slavery to freedom" (58). To him, the episode establishes that "education and slavery [are] incompatible with each other" (60), and it inspires him to get free through a gain of the ability to read and write.

Near twelve and intent on learning to wield words well, Douglass buys *The Columbian Orator*, a primer on rhetoric, from a store in Baltimore. He studies it closely. "Every opportunity I got," he recalls, "I used to read this book." The primer is full of psalms for freedom. "A dialogue between a master and his slave" (61) furnishes a good example. In the exchange, a fugitive from slavery, recaptured for the third time, is asked by his master why he continues attempting to run away since he has shown him kindness. As a human being, the slave responds, his spirit yearns for freedom, and so, no matter what, he suffers in slavery. His logic persuades his heedful master to emancipate him; it convinces Douglass that words can win liberty.

Before getting the meaning of the word "abolition," Douglass harbors doubts about his chances of enjoying freedom in American society; southern slavery has flagged the limits of his horizons. It has rendered it hard to see any public will to let him live free. However, "after a patient waiting," he says, "[he] got one of [the] city papers, containing an account of the number of petitions from the north, praying for the abolition of slavery in the District of Columbia, and of the slave trade between the states," and then it dawns on him that if he were to flee, he could find refuge. "The light broke in upon me by degrees," (62) he says. Growingly confident that he was not born to exist like an animal on a farm and sure that he could improve his status, Douglass pursues literacy more diligently than ever with an eye to trying his hand at writing. He muses, given an ability to pen words, "I might have occasion to write my own pass." In sum, he becomes obsessed with literacy, as he dreams that the skill will enable him to book his own passage to freedom. "Thus, after a long, tedious effort for years," he remembers, "I finally succeeded in learning how to write" (63).

In the long run, Douglass's devotion to educating himself pays big dividends. It awakens in him a wish for freedom and keeps it alive during his stay on Covey's farm, where, though most wretched, he eyes scores of ships with white sails aloft, "moving off to the mighty ocean" (74), across the bright bosom of the Chesapeake Bay, and feels impelled to utter:

You are loosed from your moorings, and are
free; I am fast in my chains, and am a slave!
You move merrily before the gentle gale, and I
sadly before the bloody whip! You are freedom's swift-winged angels, that fly round the
world; I am confined in bands of iron! O that I
were free! O, that I were on one of your gallant decks, and under your protecting wing!
Alas, betwixt me and you, the turbid waters
roll. Go on, go on. O that I could also go!
Could I but swim! (74-75)

The consciousness stirs him to rebel against Covey; it later
spurs him to achieve proficiency at caulking in Baltimore
which permits him to cut a deal with his master that affords
him a decent measure of freedom. "My pathway became
much more smooth than before," he reports; "my condition
was now much more comfortable" (93). It positions him for
flight. Thereafter, although he expects to find work as a
caulker in New Bedford, following his arrival there, "such
[is] the strength of prejudice against color, among white
calkers that they [refuse] to work with [him]," and so to his
dismay he can "get no employment" (103) in the trade. Yet,
in 1841, his verbal skill proves dazzling and draws the
notice of Garrisonians who offer him gainful employment
as a lecturer in the abolitionist movement, and thereafter
he conducts his own affairs swimmingly.

   An American Slave conforms to the epic structure
of the *Autobiography*. The slave narrative opens with a
humble start, plagued by oppression. It stars a man who
uses knowledge to gain freedom and prosperity. Like the
other tale, Douglass's story ends with the main character
involved in public service housing the hope of helping others help themselves to realize their potential. It could be
labeled an imitation, if it were not true that Douglass was
ignorant of Franklin's manuscript during the time at
which the black man composed his personal history; along
with the vast majority of the general public, he lacked
access to Franklin's book, until 1868, when John Bigelow
printed his edition of the volume in the United States.

   It is fair to assert that *An American Slave* at birth
represented what literary critic Claudio Guillen would

term "the ultraindividual point of view" (1971, 345) within the moral boundaries of the country. Guillen understood that each and every society in the world banks on shared understandings. Indeed, without a common sense of the world, a collective lacks sufficient latitude to reach above the chaotic state inhabited by the chastened builders of the Tower of Babel. Social orders center on codes conjured by convictions striking most natives as music and aliens as noise. Supporting such strictures solicits sympathy in every segment of a social order since it substantiates the chief outlook with pinpoint precision in the confines of surrounding circles. Douglass's book has that sort of significance in American literary culture. Within his milieu, the story harbored the import of a bright lookout from a crow's nest, conveying the degree to which the ship of state sailed on course.

Sadly, *An American Slave* has had its local merits clouded. Racial measures have cast shadows of doubt over its gravity. Critics have restricted the book's scope to a spot planted on a bank of the mainstream. They have rated it a cultural expression differing in a radical fashion from standard modes, for it issues from a black source; a number have failed to recognize the text as a classic social product. Social blinders have persuaded them that major writers who expressed their "latent conviction" in the nineteenth century and thereby related "the universal sense" (Emerson 1983, 259) were always white. Such readers have assumed that blacks in the past lacked the aptitude to speak for more than narrow concerns in the land; hence, they have missed how *An American Slave* represented the national soul.

For instance, in reviewing Douglass's text, Fuller brushed aside its general importance. She never fancied it addressing more than a parochial issue. In her view, she says, the slave narrative should be "prized as a specimen of the powers of the Black Race" in the face of a widespread bias against it. Instead of embracing blacks as her equals, Fuller subscribes to the notion that they contrast whites with a quality that has them bandy words with "a torrid energy and saccharine fulness" utterly foreign to others.

Further, she finds it wise to accept that blacks have "a talent for melody, a ready skill at imitation and adaption, an almost indestructible elasticity of nature," for "the African Race [has] in them a peculiar element" (Andrews 1991, 21-23). Her analysis refrains from giving *An American Slave* credit for achieving more than the status of a soulful cry against suffering marginal to the national development.

Remarks by Dana in *Before the Mast* prove that he shared Fuller's regard for blacks. He calls the only black hand on the *Pilgrim* "a simple-hearted African" (48); with delight, he tells how the shipmate is nice to him during their journey together. The black man, who serves as the ship's cook, seems made to amuse, as he forever strives to please his mates with bits of very lively chatter laced with superstition. Instead of a person, the black figure favors a parrot. Dana's related image of the Kanakas tribe faced in California tells that his background had set him to see various people of color in the same way. In the midst of interpreting the Kanakas as men who act and sound like apish pets, Dana says, "They have great powers of ridicule and are [impressive] mimics, many of them discovering and imitating the peculiarities of our own people before we had observed them ourselves" (210). With the white writer Fuller, he suspected that individuals with dark skin can be said to approximate adorable little signifying monkeys less than reasonable creatures, and in the process he unveiled the typical stereotype of African Americans.

In contrast, Douglass offers himself as a rational identity conforming to the norm; he reflects conventional wisdom without being a fluke. Akin to a priest, the author imparts counsel in his address, called "Self-Made Men," which sanctified the prevailing morality of the day. The text verifies that Douglass had absorbed the zeitgeist and was set to divulge it. Really his most popular speech, it was first presented in 1859, and "the last known delivery" occurred at an industrial school for native Indians in Pennsylvania over thirty years later. John Blassingame, with John McKivigan, observes that the lecture was given over and over again totaling "more than fifty times to

audiences across the United States" with few revisions
(1992, 545-46). The sermon rests on the premise that there
exists a class of "men" who merit recognition for having
hewn "out for themselves a way to success" (1992, 550). It
finds the social order "to be preeminently the home and
patron" of such people due to "the conditions in which [it]
originated" (569).

Douglass represents the self-made man as a person
who has profited from learning. He preaches that he has
"attained knowledge" that has empowered him to build his
"own good fortunes." The trope of a swimmer cast from a
ship at sea substantiates the argument. "Flung overboard
in the midnight storm on the broad and tempest-tossed
ocean of life, [shoved off] without ropes, planks, oars or
life-preservers," Douglass says, he has "bravely buffeted
the frowning billows and [has] risen in safety and life
where others, supplied with the best appliances for safety
and success," have swooned, sobbed and then sunk into
oblivion. Douglass goes on to say that a self-made man
"need not claim to be a hero," yet and still, there exists a
real nobility in his tenacity "and something of sublimity
and [splendor] in his triumph" (Blassingame 1992, 55).

The heroic type is a product of "self-culture." His
fruition stems from "well directed, honest toil." Douglass
observes, "It is surprising with what small means, in the
field of earnest effort, great results have been achieved"
(Blassingame and McKivigan 1992, 565). "I do not think
much," he states, "of the accident or good luck theory of
self-made men" (552). He insists, "Without culture there
can be no growth" (555). The world is crowded with men
"who make but little headway in life" for want of a steady
aim; too many "never get beyond the outer bark of an
idea," from a want of resolution "to dig to the core" (560).
Like flowers, "self-made men" sprout in the world from
"persistent devotion . . . to work and to the acquisition of
knowledge" (565). Douglass guesses, "Every instance of
such success is an example and a help to humanity" (550).

The author admits that human beings are unborn
as islands intended to survive without ties to any others.
"Properly speaking," he says, "there are in the world no

such men as self-made men." In actuality, "Our best and most valued acquisitions have been obtained" from some of our fellows or forefathers in fields of inquiry and information. To Douglass, willpower alone cannot "lift a man into absolute independence of his fellow-men." He says, "I believe in individuality, but individuals are, to the mass, like waves to the ocean." His statement signals that private fortunes, to a big extent, are tailored by the constitution of a culture. "We differ as the waves," he contends, "but are one as the sea" (549). Douglass means that in life, circumstances sway prospects; it takes a fair blend of choice and chance for people to reach their stride.

He predicts that the future will prove bright for the average citizen as long as the country remains true to its origins. The land springs from a mind to let "all doors fly open" (569) to private initiative, he attests in his speech. It is the property of folks who see themselves with "no past and very little present," but a future of great promise. By design, a culture that "saves itself the trouble of looking up a [person's] kinsfolks in order to determine his [post] in life and the [parcel] of respect due him" (570), the nation holds that what matters most "is not so much what has been, or what is now, but what is to be" in the future. Therefore, inclined to honor ability over ancestry, unlike ancient cultures, where "men, on all sides, endeavor to continue from youth to old age in their several callings and to abide in their several stations" (571) settled at birth, American society, "an ever moving mass" (572), urges "every man as he comes upon the stage of active life, 'Now do your level best!' 'Help yourself!' 'Put your shoulder to the wheel!' 'Make your own record!' 'Paddle your own canoe!' 'Be the [master] of your own fortune!'" (570). The actual "moral atmosphere" was cast to harbor a state of liberty for all "men" to pursue their own happiness. "In this respect," Douglass argues, "America is not [simply] the exception to the general rule, but the social wonder of the world" (571), favoring "the sea in its power and grandeur, and in the equalities of its particles" (572).

In the speech, it saddens Douglass that blacks have been thought to lack the necessities to warrant a chance to do as they choose. He sees that blacks have languished at the bottom of society, for too many whites, like Jefferson, have "entertained a rather low estimate of [their merits] (566) and, as a result, have denied them fair treatment. Still, if the land were to "throw open to [blacks] the doors of the schools" and "give [them] a chance to do whatever [they] can do well" (557), Douglass supposes, a multitude would join "in lifting [their] race" to marvelous ranks (566) and would demonstrate that discovering a causeway open to advantage "is the most potent factor" (569) related to achievement. He turns up good examples in the lives of individuals like Benjamin Banneker, "a man of African descent" and "learned mathematician" who worked "to lay out the city of Washington" (566), in addition to William Dietz, "a black man of Albany" (567) and civil engineer whose plan for a railroad was published in the *Scientific American*. Douglass presents the citations with the hope that they will "aid to roll back the tide of [shame] and [scorn] which pride and prejudice have poured out" against blacks (567). While "it is customary to assert that [blacks] never invented anything" vital (568), he hazards, they have been innovative for a very long time and, given "fair play" (557), any one of them could prosper well in American society.

Enterprises generated by a reverence for learning teemed in circles including the ex-slave Douglass and his contemporary black Americans. In magnitude, his vision mirrored the outlook among his peers with African roots. Focused on the idea that learning can supply room for freedom, blacks, hounded by the specter of slavery, eyed despotism as a corrupt occupation. To them, young minds very much favored fertile gardens with a potency to sprout achievement in the light of freedom. They guessed that books, stored in libraries and handled in schools, served as vital tools for success. Through mental cultivation, blacks trusted, their offspring could quite naturally bask in liberty.

Reemploying the shape of the U.S. Constitution, in 1829 David Walker published his *Appeal*. It was a typical bit of black thought when it appeared. In its Preamble,

Walker laments that blacks in the country "are the most degraded, wretched, and abject set of beings that ever lived since the world began" (Brawley [1953] 1970, 125) due to an extreme lack of knowledge enforced by severe prejudice hypocritical in "this *Republican Land of Liberty*" (127). The *Appeal* refers to black slavery as the result of a prevalent suspicion among whites that blacks are born for use as mere beasts of burden despite the fact that ingenious men and women, resembling his fellow blacks in physical appearance, conceived and constructed the monuments of ancient Egypt, the cradle of Western civilization. Walker argues that the prejudice has lured legislators into making it against the law "that a person of color should receive an education" (142), and so most blacks have fallen at the mercy of whites, for social relations have transformed the darker citizens into creatures as dumb as mules. Walker vouches that blacks have as just a claim to "manhood" and citizenship as anyone. He meant that his own kind, like all "men," absolutely have a natural reason and social right to captain their own fates through the application of learning.

The model individual depicted by Douglass in his noted work recovered the ideal person, whom, according to Walker, blacks merited a chance to actualize. Between 1820 and 1860, echoes of the conviction arose ceaselessly in black groups. During 1853, a teacher named Charles Reason, seeking public support for black education, voiced the understanding. In his statement, Reason proclaims that "the free-colored man," along with "his bond-brother," just wanted "self-provision," a condition of dignity and delight (Aptheker 1951, 362) natural in character and available through individual culture. Earlier, in the spring of 1831, a convention in the City of Brotherly Love pleaded "for mental cultivation" (117) in the black community with the insistence that "knowledge is power" (118). Two years later, several black men in the city organized and founded a library called the Philadelphia Library Company of Colored Persons; they acted on the notion that it was prudent to provide their "rising youth" access to "a proper cultivation for literary pursuits and the improvement of the faculties and powers of their minds" (138). In addition, an 1841 study of the black Americans in Philadelphia reports that they took learning "as one important avenue" to happiness and in consequence had formed "numerous literary associations" (213). Many nineteenth-century manuscripts manifest that blacks, like Douglass and Walker, believed, "The educated man—the man of a cultivated taste, whose mind is enriched with stores of useful knowledge" (Porter 1971, 164) meant them at their best.

Gates detects this heritage of esteem for learning in his *Signifying Monkey* on black literature. But his study suffers from a shallow sense of history. Although he sees that "it is to the literature of the black slave that the critic must turn to identify" the birth and breeding of black letters (1988, 127), he envisions a lack of input from African forefathers (129) that is illustrative of African American thought and has been influential in Western literary culture prior to the dawn of the Enlightenment; he hints that every class in all early African communities was full of illiterates; it never dawns on him that Arabic was written and read throughout West Africa when Timbuktu was a center of learning loaded with libraries held sacred by a rich ruling class; he never notes how Islam spread learning through Africa and raised the University of Sankore during the Dark Ages; the scholar leads his audience to suspect that the idea of writing never crossed a single black mind in Africa until white Christian missionaries reach the "dark continent" in boats bearing books that the whites would use to train the natives to make themselves more significant than monkeys; he fails to uncover literacy as an indigenous presence in Africa prior to European invasions; he implicates that blackness is a biological condition bereft in isolation of the intensity and ingenuity to invent and interpret instruments with which to script abstractions of life for generations of study; his statements insinuate that a silver lining in the dark cloud of slavery over the heads of early blacks in the country was a great chance to pick up reading and writing from naturally lettered white men with a tremendous talent for working with words; it is especially unfortunate that Gates overlooks how *The Confessions of St. Augustine* (c. A.D. 400), the prototype in form for the slave narrative, stems from the brain of a Numidian man, while *Don Quixote* (1605), the forerunner in content for the black genre, remakes a grand Moorish tradition.[8] So, noting that for black people "writing became the visible sign, the commodity of exchange, the text and technology of reason," the critic combs through many slave narratives from *A Narrative of*

---

8. It is generally assumed that St. Augustine was white, if not dark white. Much of the popular view is based on a portrait of the man, the saint, the author of Christian theology, painted by the Renaissance Italian artist Botticelli over a millennium after the death of the Numidian. St. Augustine was born in Thagaste, a spot in modern Algeria. At the time (A.D. 354), Romans in the late years of their empire occupied the territory with a multi-colored force, centuries after Herodotus attributed black faces and woolly heads to the neighboring Egyptians. It stands to reason that mating practices uninhibited by color prejudice caused the local hues to resemble the ebony-to-ivory spectrum that marks the mix of Americans of African descent, that is, a range running somewhere between black and light black. In other words, if light black Sally Hemings, the enslaved half sister to Jefferson's wife, was *black*, then in all likelihood so was St. Augustine. The thought that "the father of Christianity" was black or light black leads more often than not these days to cognitive dissonance.

There is also a preoccupation with imagining the Moors as whites or dark whites. The wish conforms to the impulse to whitewash history. The group did consist of Berbers who probably were *white*. But the name for the body of people was derived from the ancient Greek word for barbarian or foreigner because they were aliens in North Africa who migrated there about 4000 years ago and were dominated in succession by Carthaginians, Romans, and Vandals. Many of them must have turned black or light black over time from miscegenation. In any event, they never made up the bulk of the population along the African shores of the Mediterranean sea; most of the inhabitants favored in appearance the majority in Brazil today: black or light black. The latter played the biggest part in the era between A.D. 718 and A.D. 1492 when African empires reigned in glory and Spain was swayed by Moors, or what Christians called Muslims, who constituted a mix of people from the lip of Asia that kisses North Africa and more often from the bosom of the sands and savannahs that embrace Africa. These black and light black people provided Europe with translations of the lost works of Aristotle and influenced Cervantes as jazz influenced T. S. Eliot.

For more details, see Paul Bohannan's *Africa and Africans* (Natural History Press, 1964), George James's *Stolen Legacy* (Africa World Press, 1992), Winthrop Jordan's *White over Black* (Penguin, 1969), Joel A. Rogers's *Sex and Race* (H. M. Rogers, 1967) with his *World's Great Men of Color* (Macmillan, 1972), Frank Snowden's *Before Color Prejudice* (Harvard University Press, 1983), and Ivan Van Sertima's *They Came before Columbus*. While these texts are open to debate at points, they nevertheless invoke a vision of our Western heritage as a colorful drama in which more than just white men have played major parts.

*the Most Remarkable Particulars in the Life of James
Albert Ukawsaw Gronniosaw, an African Prince* (1774) to
Douglass's *An American Slave* and finds at their nerve
center "the trope of a Talking Book," a black idealization
of literacy full of awe. The inquiry leads Gates to imply
that being literate was an uncharacteristic pursuit for
folks of African descent. His criticism alleges that "the
mastery of Western letters" (165) typified "the elements of
wonder that the young African encounter[ed] on his road to
Western culture" (155). At the time, blind to the measure to
which comedies from the Carthaginian Terence (c. B.C.
190-59) created characters for Shakespeare's plays and yet
to discover literate Africans like Ahmed Baba, whose prose
in the 1500s captured the mind in Songhay, or ignorant of
the black Russian Alexander Pushkin, whose rich poetry
(particularly *Eugene Onegin*, issued in 1833) arrested the
Russian imagination, and blind to the colored Frenchmen
Alexander Dumas, whose tales (such as *The Three Mus-
keteers*, printed in 1844) won the French heart, Gates connotes that Douglass and his black fellows were unsuited to
uphold national ideals in letters.[9] His *Signifying Monkey*
implies that the history of writing from people with African
ancestry commenced a short time ago within a circle of
slaves standing in the position of pioneers prone to forge a
brand of script identifiable as "the text of blackness" (128),

---

9. The theory here is that all the men mentioned were *black*. If Douglass, with a
father who descended from Europeans and a mother who descended from Africans,
was black, then Pushkin who had Abyssinian and Russian ancestors was black, too, and
so was Dumas who had a mixed Haitian ancestry along with Terence who came from a
North African blend of humanity. Hearing that these men were black would not raise
our eyebrows if we were not trained to see white men standing alone as the stars of
Western history. To maintain the myth, we are inclined to view North Africa as a European outpost strictly populated by whites since the first pyramid appeared by the Nile,
and to think that the African general Hannibal who humbled Rome during the Punic
Wars had to be white along with the Moors who dominated Spain before the Spanish
Inquisition because, like Terence and St. Augustine, they were outstanding. We over-
look the fact that Shakespeare who was much closer in time to ancient Africa than we
are called the Moors in *The Merchant of Venice* and *Othello* black and used tawny to
describe Cleopatra in his *Antony and Cleopatra*. In our era racked by racism, we have
imagined that the casting of Elizabeth Taylor as the Egyptian queen in the movie *Cleopatra* was realistic because the Hollywood actress is white.

a type of rare cogitation countering the mainstream; but, a broad sense of history proves the idea false.

An American Slave is not foreign matter. It is a match for *Before the Mast*. Both works revolve around a common theme. They tie majesty to the triumph of liberty through the use of learning and grant all "men" the reason as well as the right to pursue that end; they are equally very legendary in the land. Solely a shade of difference in tone divides them. The shift clones the sort of nuance that splits dialects. Douglass's narrative by its tone differs from Dana's story as a cry against a flogging released by a victim stands out from a protest issued by a witness. With a distinct intensity, an intelligence missing from the motif in *Before the Mast* accents the message sealed in the pages of *An American Slave*; relatively speaking, beautifully, in sum, the two books make the same point through modulated pitches.

4

Jacob's Ladder

In the field of human values, women such as Fanny Fern and Harriet Jacobs abided by common grounds during the nineteenth century. From where they stood, the world turned with a rhythm close to the motion of the sea. Their outlook set people everywhere in the same boat. Mental cultivation, they professed, could book anyone a first-class passage through life. Yet, they lamented, a rule of thumb, dating from no later than the time of Aristotle, threatened to drown them in sorrow by dragging them to the level of an empty sack doomed to sink into idleness between recurrent bouts of labor for others. With aplomb, *Ruth Hall* (1855) and *Incidents in the life of a Slave Girl* (1861), respectively written by Fern and Jacobs, manifest the related vision.

If neither author had ever written her book, it would be possible to deduce their shared ethical sense from the fruits of their separate lives. Relatives of gifted kin, the women lost their mothers at the advent of times that tried their souls. In later years, they braved tyranny at the hands of men who saw them as items made for use. Yet, literacy empowered them to improve their lots. Writing won them prominence and released them to harvest a range of liberty pioneering in reach.

Fern started as Sara Payson Willis in Maine, on July 9, 1811. Her family history made it logical to expect literary success from her. Following her birth, her father, Nathaniel Willis, Jr., the son of a journalist, moved his young family to Boston, where in 1816 he founded the nation's first religious newspaper; in 1827, he launched another publication devised to instruct and entertain youth. During the latter year, Fern's brother, Nathaniel P. Willis, eager to follow in his father's footsteps, graduated from Yale, printed a collection of poetry entitled *Sketches*, and embarked on a career in publishing. As Joyce W. Warren recognizes, Fern was convinced that any poetry in her nature came from her mother, Hannah Parker, who, harboring it, could have used the talent to achieve some distinction in "literary pursuits," if she had been ready to break from household chores (1986, xi) and concentrate on writing.

Although Fern went to the Ladies Seminary before going to Catherine Beecher's Hartford Female Seminary, where she met female authors like Lydia Sigourney and Catherine Maria Sedgwick, she was never urged at home to pursue a career in writing. In school she developed excellent verbal skills; she proved to be especially good at satire. From the time that she turned twelve, her father was happy to have her give him a hand by reading proofs and writing pieces for his newspapers (Warren 1986, xii). Nevertheless, her father who ruled the roost believed that the point of Fern's education was to teach her tasks that would help her to wait on others. Therefore, he preferred for her to focus her attention on household chores, such as baking and sewing, with an aim to become a wonderful wife and mother. It appeared that she would live up to his expectations once she married Charles Elredge, the son of a physician, with a job in banking.

Seven years into a cheerful marriage that produced three daughters, Fern was suddenly shaken by the death of her mother. The event occurred at the start of a stormy phase that would plant her on a path that would shock her father and brother. Inside of two years, in the wake of her mother's passing, Fern's oldest daughter died and was followed by her husband, who left her bankrupt. She tried to support herself by sewing but found it impossible to make ends meet. When she turned to the men in her family for assistance, they treated her as a worry that they were impatient to unload on someone else. Introducing an edition of *Ruth Hall*, Susan Belasco Smith establishes that terribly "griefstricken and unable to make a living as a seamstress or secure a position as a teacher," poor Fern married Samuel Farrington, a widower, in 1849. It was strictly a marriage of convenience arranged to promote her own "social and financial security" (Fern [1855] 1997, xxvii). But she decided to walk out of his life at the end of two long years because she refused to let him bully her as he was prone to do; in reply, he divorced Fern on the grounds of desertion, and she sought to make a living as a writer.

Having mastered the power of literacy in school, Fern used it to climb to great heights. Her ascent hardly happened itself without pain and perseverance. Unable to feed both of her surviving daughters, she was compelled to send the older girl to live with her in-laws. Then too, she faced a mountain of rejections from publishers, including her own brother. Fern nevertheless grew more and more determined to become an independent career woman with enough money to care for her children. Dwelling in cheap boarding houses, without much more than bread for food, whenever and however possible, Fern penned pieces with a plan to publish them in area newspapers. In 1851, Fern broke into print with an editorial in the *Olive Branch*; a year later, she had her own column and "thus became the first woman" to accomplish the feat in the country (Warren xv). Nancy Walker attests that Fern became "the most widely reprinted and most highly paid newspaper columnist of the 1850's" (Walker 1993, 1); she proved popular enough to sell collections of her articles in addition to a second novel, *Rose Clark* (1856).

Beyond bringing her fame and fortune, her work enriched other lives. Her subjects concerned women, but they contained a spirit important to the whole nation. "She urged women," Warren says, "to broaden their experience when they could, through [learning] and a career or simply by reading and writing" (1986, xxxiii). Fern implored her female readers to trust that they were born on an equal footing with men and so were able to enjoy liberty through the use of learning. Mostly, Fern resorted to irony in order to make her point. "Borrowed Light," her 1853 article that appeared in the *True Flag*, on April 9, with a few words for aspiring women writers, typifies her general approach. In the piece, the author holds that a woman "fully persuaded that [her] destiny lies undeveloped in an inkstand" (i.e. a woman who wishes to write) would succeed if she strove to ape current conventions, for an attempt at originality would result in "an immensity of trouble," because of her frivolous nature; yet, Fern means to leave the opposite impression; like a ship sailing "under false colors" to mask its purpose, she exercised sarcasm in her piece to conceal her feeling that every woman is equipped to "light a torch of their own" (Warren 1986, 252), a gift with which to shine in the world. Fern's sentiments harmonized with the eighteenth-century rage for equality that fired the American Revolution and welded the country together.

Fern's view would never have drawn a fuss from Jacobs. In a chat about women and writing, the two were bound to agree, and, in truth, they may have a few times, since, twice serving Fern's brother, as a nursemaid for his children, Jacobs became acquainted with Fern.[1] In light of the fact that both of them embraced an ambition to write which went unendorsed and unencouraged by Fern's older brother, they were able to concur that such treatment was unfair. In contrast to the opinion of Fern's sibling, each woman saw writing as a skill that a woman, given interest and training, could master for profit as well as the average man. From the tenor of Jacobs's life, you can tell that in private, she would have praised Fern for finding in ordinary women the potential to write and comparing the

---

1. In "Domesticity and the Economics of Independence," which appears in *The (Other) American Traditions* (New Brunswick, NJ: Rutgers University Press, 1993.), the editor, J. W. Warren, reports that a diary by Thomas Butler Gunn connects the women. See page 84 in the book for details.

endowment to an inner light, fueled by learning, with which they could leave their mark.

About two years younger than Fern, as Jean Fagan Yellin found, Jacobs was born to slaves in Edenton, North Carolina. Her folks were proud and inventive people who never cottoned to slavery. Based on her ancestry, it was logical to expect her to conduct herself in an intelligent and independent manner. Her father, Elijah, was a carpenter; with the trade, he put himself in a position to gain control over a measure of his time by hiring out his services to different bidders. The woman's mother, Delilah, who died when Jacobs was six, left the impression of a regal figure, desirous of the best for her children, consisting of Jacobs and her younger brother, John, who would flee ultimately bondage early in his adult life to emerge as a well known abolitionist. Jacobs's maternal grandmother, named Molly Horniblow, personified the family character. Misbegotten black daughter of a South Carolina slaveholder, Molly was a pillar of strength and mother of five children, respected throughout Edenton for expedience and enterprise; her demeanor led a white neighbor to purchase and free her, and the woman, in turn, dedicated herself to baking biscuits at midnight for sale with the hope of raising enough cash to emancipate all of her children; in the case of her youngest son, her dream came true. With such relations to guide her, Jacobs could never have taken slavery for granted.

Jacobs's mettle began being put to the test around puberty, when her slave mistress passed away. Then, she was assigned to the daughter of James Norcom and taken into his household. Her father died a year later; Norcom, a licentious man, thereafter started prodding her to consider her body his possession not hers. At sixteen, prohibited by the man from marrying a free, young black who loved her and choosing to resist the slaveholder's wish to have her serve him as a concubine, Jacobs crept into an affair with Samuel Tredwell Sawyer, which produced a boy and a girl, Joseph and Louisa Matilda. In order to punish her for opposing his will, Norcom banished her to working in the fields on his plantation; he was resolved to weaken her stance against him. She never minded him; assisted by friends and family, she went into hiding. In her efforts to elude the evil man, Jacobs moved from being secluded in a snaky swamp for a dark night to cramping up in a stuffy garret occupied by rats and mice in her grandmother's roof for seven lonely, painful years. Stoically, she bore these ordeals, for she was not ready to let anyone master her; she felt too equal to everyone else.

Learning supplied her with relief from the solitude and sorrow that plagued her retreat. As things turned out, it was good that she had learned to read and write during her childhood. In her *Slave Girl*,[2] Jacobs thanks her first mistress for permitting her to pick up literacy. The skill enabled her to expel gloom by deciphering the Bible in her hideaway. Moreover, it allowed her to write a letter and have it mailed from a New York site to fool Norcom into supposing that she was settling in Boston when, in fact, she was still secreted in her grandmother's loft. By the trick, she freed herself to slip downstairs in the house and stretch her limbs for a spell, to ward off physical paralysis, without being apprehended by Norcom.

Jacobs had the strength to don a disguise and sail to Philadelphia in 1842. In the wake of her discreet passage from the South, she dove into a stubborn pursuit of self-sufficiency from New York to Boston and back. She was set on unearthing ways and means to support herself and her children, with whom she would eventually be reunited by her own arrangements. Prepared to take any decent job that she could land, Jacobs initiated her northern quest by sewing and baby-sitting for others. Meanwhile she spent her spare time on reading and writing. Her labors paid off. In her words, she "improved [her] mind" from the day that she "first arrived in Philadelphia" (Jacobs [1861] 1973, xiii) until she qualified herself to run the Rochester Anti-slavery Office and Reading Room located on top of the shop from which Frederick Douglass published his paper, the *North Star*. Her climb in society put her in touch with the

---

2. Henceforth, I use this abbreviation for *Incidents in the Life of a Slave Girl*.

feminist Amy Post; the white female activist convinced her to write her *Slave Girl*.

Jacobs sat herself down to start her book in 1853 and it was 1858 before she got an actual chance to finish it. Societal and monetary checks curtailed her opportunities to do more than sneak a moment now and then "to scratch [herself] a few lines" (Yellin 1987, 234). Before finishing her slave narrative, she drew some attention by publishing several letters against slavery in the New York *Tribune*. Nevertheless, it was hard to find a publisher for her book. "Little dreaming of the time that might elapse" (246) prior to seeing her story in print, she canvassed for three trying years to turn up a company primed to put out her work. *A Slave Girl* notwithstanding secured her international fame. Her ensuing lot grew more and more fruitful.

Public service consumed a big part of her later life. While the Civil War racked the nation, Jacobs traveled to the south to clothe, feed, and teach black refugees from the depths of slavery. At the end of the national crisis, she went on lending a hand to ex-slaves in need of assistance to make the most of their newfound freedom. The social work took her back to old Edenton, North Carolina, her birth-place, where she inherited her grandmother's property and sold it for a tidy sum. Her activities also carried her to Savannah, Georgia, as well as London, England. Upbeat, she stayed the course until her final days, when she played a part in the birth of the National Association of Colored Women.

Having died in 1897, Jacobs outlived Fern by close to three decades. Their careers, though, achieved a kindred grandeur. Contesting paradoxical local customs, each found her way in the world without stooping to others. Jacobs never knew marriage. Remembering the death of her first husband and her divorce from her second one, Fern married a third and final time, but only after her fiance had agreed to sign a prenuptial agreement that left her in charge of her own finances. Their marital choices defied entrenched social standards that expected women to depend on matrimony for their personal welfare. By suc-ceeding without succumbing to the prevailing wifely lot,

the life of both Jacobs and Fern invited reform by representing women as model citizens of epic proportions.

The general notion of women, being a discrepancy
in social thought, denied that their histories could achieve
the standing of a national epic about a figure who used his
wits to move up in the world. For her own good, the public
assumed, Barbara Welter notes, that every woman should
abide by "the cult of true womanhood" and mind a man.
Welter confirms in *Dimity Convictions* that the prevalent
image of women imputed that they could attain "happiness
and power" exclusively through a pious devotion to chasti-
ty, subservience, and a home-oriented existence directed
by a male (1976, 21-39). Basically, the story of a great woman, from the given point of view, was bound to recount little
more than household chores performed with great care by a
polite wife who lived to honor and obey a proud husband.
An absurd chauvinism sanctioned the perception. At heart,
it upheld an ancient bias against women that rated them
inferior to men due to a want of reason.

Aristotle recorded that kind of partiality in his
Politics. His book proclaims without the slightest bit of hesitation that an interplay of superior and inferior forces
turns the world. Every sound association, he asserts,
involves a compound of dual elements with one set to be
served by the other. According to the Greek philosopher,
"The world would be a curious place if it did not include
some [entities] meant to be free, as well as some that are
meant to be" ruled (286). Concerning people, Aristotle says,
they too divide into one of the dichotomies based on the
degree to which someone possesses a measure of reason,
that is actually, "the ability to exercise forethought" (3).
Judging the consummate man a reasonable creature,
Aristotle observes that a lot of men are born devoid of
rationality and as a result are destined to tender their bet-
ters "bodily help in meeting [their] daily requirements"
(13). More pertinently, he says, "the female and the slave
occupy the same position" (3); he means that women are
missing forethought, and hence their relation to rational
men is "that of the superior to the inferior—of the ruling to

the ruled" (13); men are designed to direct women, "except where there is some departure from nature" (32).

From Aristotle's vantage point, the heart of "moral goodness" (36) differs between men and women. While he allowed that virtue is a latent attribute in humans, he thought that it involved opposite qualities for each sex. He identified a man of nobility as a reflective person who lords over others with discretion; on the other hand, he pictured a virtuous woman as a modest creature who waits on others with fine style and grace. This kind of sexual classification failed to log an actual advance in human reasoning. It just transmitted a worldwide standard. A cursory review of sexual relations throughout the length and breath of recorded history unfailingly demonstrates that civilizations customarily rated women inferior to men, due to a proposed female mindlessness classifying them at their best in service to males.

In ancient Sumerian society, where patriarchy let a husband reign over " both his relatives and his slaves," a popular historian noticed "a pattern which was until very recently observable in most parts of the world" (Roberts 1993, 44). Evidence suggests that Egyptian women had freedom and stature in the ruling classes; "some women were literate" and wore an official title "for a female scribe" (64). Elsewhere, women were very much less privileged. "In classical Greece girls were thought" unfit to learn and on the average they faced a life of drudgery (153). Islamic lands ranked women below men (273), along with traditional Hindu communities that embraced "the practice of *suttee*, or self-immolation of widows on their husbands' funeral pyres" (344). Due to a Chinese disregard for the feminine gender, "in hard times girl babies were exposed by poor families to die," and as a rule a "high-born lady," eyed as a doll for male amusement, was apt to be crippled by foot-binding (361). In Africa during the Dark Ages, when the empires of Ghana, Mali, and Songhay, flourished in succession and overflowed with a reverence for learning, the conventional reading of the sexes placed men in charge of women and mandated death or enslavement for adulterous wives, but no penalties for wayward husbands. It was not better for women in Medieval Europe. On the continent at that time, "whether they were of noble or common blood [most] women suffered, by comparison with the menfolk, from important legal and social disabilities" (415).

Not long ago, Susan Harris detected the recurring slant, relegating women to a post below men, in the culture and early criticism of nineteenth-century American society. For example, she invited her audience to take Fred Lewis Pattee's *The Feminine Fifties* (1940) as a faithful echo of the regard for women in the middle of the last millennium. The critic found that the study revives the idea that males and females differ in constitution, as it contends that women, unlike men, are irrational and their writings, impotent to do more than dish out sentimentality, fostered an era of emotional excess in the 1850s when literature written by them was very much in vogue (Harris 2-3). Harris also determined that Fern knew what reservations faced women during the decade that greeted the heralded "American Renaissance." She illustrated that the author of *Ruth Hall* knew that "Women were especially associated with feeling" (114) and solely expected to gain fulfillment "through the agency of a male" (117). Fern, Harris reveals, used irony in the novel, in effect, a fake sentimental voice to check an obscene custom decreeing, women had to answer to men because they were too emotional to manage their own affairs.

A perception of doubts that women have the talent to be their own mistresses looms on page after page of *Ruth Hall*. A worthwhile instance arises in the portrayal of the protagonist as a dreadful misfit among the girls at the boarding school operated by Madame Moreau. Marked by a fondness for "being alone by herself" (Fern [1855] 1997, 4) as well as a passion for music and poetry, Ruth is judged queer by her schoolmates, who act serious about books in the presence of Madame Moreau but really just want to win men's hearts. Deeming writing as a "frightful task," the girls are arrested by "amazement and admiration" (6) at the ease with which Ruth writes, and woefully they turn to her for help whenever they need an essay. Otherwise, they regard her as if she were a freak of nature, constantly bothering "her head with stupid books," while daily growing more and more attractive, "and all the world [knows]," her peers declares, "that it [is] quite unnecessary for a pretty woman to be clever" (7).

The school girls, quick to neglect their studies, "put on their bonnets and shawls, and slip out at the side-street door to meet expectant lovers" (5), patently conform to the contemporary stereotype of their gender as unreasonable creatures whose happiness nests itself in paying homage to men and gathering their bearings from them. At the time that *Ruth Hall* appeared, women were expected to aim merely to make men proud to be served by them. It was the only type of conduct that was supposed to confer on females confidence and composure. That assumption was upheld by ordinances that permitted husbands to treat their wives as their property, like a pliant instrument, if not a pretty ornament, destined for a hollow life until engaged by an eligible patron. The circumstances prove that "the young ladies at Madame Moreau's school" (6) introduce an ironic tension into Fern's novel by placing the protagonist in direct contrast to her peers and the tradition that they symbolize.

Since her mother has passed away and left her in the custody of her father and brother, Ruth's relationship with her mother-in-law, known as Mrs. Hall, implies that she becomes a poor wife, for she suffers from the absence of a proper role model during her formative years. It is obvious from the older woman's obsession with telling Ruth how to act. The memory of her unadorned wedding is fresh in the newlywed's mind when Mrs. Hall begins to find fault with her. Ruth's husband's mother alleges that she has not been "brought up properly" because she has not learned, according to the older woman, "all that a girl should learn" (12) about the business of good housekeeping before getting married. Throughout her marriage to Harry, she is intensively berated by her mother-in-law, who commands her to read, if idle, practical literature in lieu of imaginative letters, "novels and such trash" (14), for example, but spend the bulk of her time on domestic matters with a willing heart.

Fern's work demonstrates how the tenets espoused by "the cult of true womanhood" caused women to devalue mental cultivation. The persuasion conditioned them to put all of their eggs in a single basket: the prospect of marrying well. It spurred them to practice being obliging rather than assertive. Under the circumstances, aspiring to be "your own mistress" (24) was sure to fetch a woman dishonor. It was imperative for a member of Fern's sex to set her sights on home life, seem witless, and display self-effacement in order to earn respect from others.

Identifying *Ruth Hall* as a strongly nonconformist woman's story against the tides of nineteenth-century sexism, Warren brackets the book with *A Slave Girl* (Warren 1993, 84). Yellin's research has validated the claim by finding that the black work, "shaped by the empowering impulse that created the American Renaissance" (Yellin 1987, xiii), features "a new kind of female hero" (xiv) who opposes patriarchy. Hazel Carby reaches a comparable conclusion in her book *Reconstructing Womanhood* as she positions the protagonist, Linda Brent, in *A Slave Girl* "outside the parameters of the conventional heroine" (1987, 59). Indeed, the study identifies Jacobs's publication as "the most sophisticated, sustained narrative dissection of the conventions of true womanhood by a black author before emancipation" (47) and thereby links it to *Ruth Hall*. Between the lines of *A Slave Girl*, there is a lot of evidence that such a hypothesis is possibly tenable. The slave narrative harbors scores of protests against the status of contemporary women, captured by Fern.

In *A Slave Girl*, Linda's memory of Mrs. Flint, "a second wife, many years the junior of her husband," Dr. Flint, "the hoary-headed miscreant" (Jacobs [1861] 1973, 33), imparts an objection to the usual treatment of women; regretfully, it hints, allotted gender roles were corrupting female lives in every social class, including nominally the most privileged ones. Disposed to uphold custom, Linda's mistress assumes the air of a flower, steeped in humility and naturally bred to enliven a kitchen. The

white woman lets Dr. Flint dictate her affairs. If the prevalent guidelines for women were fair, Mrs. Flint's life
would be as sweet as a Georgia peach; she would be as
happy as a child at play because she would be enjoying the
best life for which a woman could hope. But she is sad, and
her sorrow leaves her so bitter that she can sit and watch a
girl be whipped until she bleeds or stand and spit in a pot of
food to spite a hungry slave.

Mrs. Flint's grief springs from her plan to play the
part of a model wife and entitle her husband to call all the
shots. Thanks to her bent, Dr. Flint, spurred by passion,
secures a free hand to drag her through the mud. Linda
reports that he has come to father at least eleven slaves.
Mrs. Flint endures her husband's comporting himself like
a bull sowing his oats as often as possible without giving a
hoot about how much it will hurt her to meet a brown kid
bearing a resemblance to him. Through the moment, in the
chapter named "The Jealous Mistress," where Linda, still
in her teens, confesses to Mrs. Flint how Dr. Flint seeks to
seduce her, and the man's wife breaks down and cries
hard and feels martyred, *A Slave Girl* solicits a change of
mind in relation to the feminine gender. "As I went on
with my account," Linda wholly remembers, "[Mrs.
Flint's] color changed frequently, she wept, and sometimes
groaned" (32). The episode effectively divulges an authorial plan to press for a review of what it might mean to be a
true woman.

Black female histories in *A Slave Girl* signal
worst-case scenarios for the depths to which nineteenth-
century mores could lower a woman. A poignant cue is
given in the sketch of the orphan niece whose generous
inheritance from a rich uncle, leaving her secure with
seven slaves, including "a woman and her six children"
(fathered by a free black man) attracts, like a magnet to
metal, a gold digger who snakes his way into her heart and
shoves her into an early grave. Prior to wedding the mer-
cenary male, the heiress is comfortable; people think that
"the whole town [does] not contain a happier family" than
that of the slaves in accord with her influence cast to spur
them "to lead pure lives" and to profit well from "their own

industry" (50). Sanctioned by marriage laws, the man on
the make seizes control of the young lady as well as her
property once she becomes his wife; with his bride impotent
to prevent him, he tears the black family apart by selling
"the two oldest boys," handing over "one little girl" to her
mother, and depositing "the other three" in his private
quarters for his benefit, in addition to having the black
father imprisoned for defying him. The outcome shatters
the slaveholder's wife; when her end comes, she feels
"glad to close her eyes on a life which [has] been made so
[vile] by the man she loved" (51). As the narration deplores
that social conditions were bent on tossing white women
with an upper-class pedigree into dire straits, it reviles that
things were prone to plunge black females into the nastiest
spot. Specifically, the story relates that while the white
heiress endures a disregard for her feelings, her black
counterparts undergo an exploitation in which they are
handled like sacks made to please a man.

Linda reaches an early awareness of the rotten
deal facing slave women in nineteenth-century American
society resulting from the dominant image of the feminine
gender as toys or tools for the masculine sex blessed with
reason. One night, when she has been in Dr. Flint's house
around three weeks, a black male slave arrives at the door
to be suspended from a rafter in the shed, by the slavemaster's orders, "so that his feet would just escape the ground"
(11), and in that way to hang, like a pig for slaughter, till
his master has finished his tea. Linda is unable to forget
what happens next; "hundreds of blows fall, in succession," on human flesh, and chilling cries for mercy
screech from the dangling man being beaten. Although the
sufferer survives the torture, it seems miraculous in the
morning, the second that Linda sees "the cowhide still wet
with blood." Rumors prompt her to suspect that Dr. Flint
has punished the slave for naming him the father of a
"very fair" child borne by his black wife. Linda's premo-
nition proves valid months later on a day marked by Dr.
Flint's decision to sell the couple and thus rid himself of
their then-habitual quarrels. The black wife, "delivered

into the trader's hands," reminds Dr. Flint, "You *prom-ised* to treat me well," and the white man responds, "You have let your tongue run too far; damn you" (12). The events show how black slave women, sadly, were simply afforded a chance to oblige their masters.

Little wonder Valerie Smith found that "the plot of Jacobs's narrative, her journey from slavery to freedom, is punctuated by . . . structures of confinement" in literal as well as figurative terms (1987, 29). In antebellum days, American women knew little choice in their lives; their horizons were terribly hemmed by a specious measure of their natures; enslaved women were the most restricted. Every slave woman's story was predisposed by her past to convey sensations of being bound in a narrow or enclosed space. In view of the social setting, women's tales from all classes were subject to express a feeling of extreme limits. In fact, the historical record makes it tempting to think that women in general and those chained to slavery in particular were pressed to create and cultivate a culture countering the mainstream in order to improve their lot.

Evidence of the routine devaluation of women sits in an editorial written in response to the 1848 woman's rights convention held in Seneca Falls. The article calls the event a farce whose cast of characters included mainly homely spinsters, mismatched wives, and domineering types, "mannish women," as anomalous as "hens that crow," who fancied themselves without a "proper sphere" in which to dwell and focus on tasks like "nursing the babies, washing the dishes, mending stockings, and sweeping the house." It continues, "they want to fill all other posts which men are ambitious to occupy," such as occupations in law, medicine, and management. After wondering, "How did woman first become subject to man as she is now?" it decides, "By her nature," which places her along with blacks below the level of white men and thus "doomed to subjection."[3] Taking women as stuff for domestic use, the editorial confirms Angela Davis's assertion that women

---

3. The editorial, entitled "The Woman's Rights Convention—The Last Act of the Drama," appeared on September 12, 1852 in the *New York Herald*.

in the nineteenth century were deemed "destined to become appendages to their men" (32).

In *Ain't I a Woman*, bell hooks checks the record and concludes that "anti-woman sexual politics" (1982, 42) was rife in early American society. She says that while racism justified the enslavement of blacks, sexism made "the lot of the black female" (43) the most difficult in the land. Within slave communities, hooks relates, sex roles "mirrored those of patriarchal white America." As a rule, she adds, "it was the black female who cooked for the family, cleaned the hut or cabin, nursed the sick, washed and mended [every stitch of clothing], and cared for the needs of children." Overall, "enslaved black females" obeyed existing gender codes "that granted men higher status than women." In fact, "Black slave men regarded [chores] like cooking, sewing, nursing, and even minor farm labor as woman's work" (44). A most disturbing aspect of the system sprouted from its propensity to train female slaves to imagine that their chief aim should be to please men. Meaning to prove it, hooks quotes from the journal of Frances Kemble, demonstrating how sexism swayed the thinking of slave women on a Georgia plantation:

> Moreover, they have all of them a most distinct and perfect knowledge of their value to their owner as property; and a woman thinks, and not so much amiss that the more frequently she adds to the number of her master's livestock by bringing new slaves into the world, the more claims she will have upon his consideration and good will. (41)

The passage demolishes any room to doubt that the popular attitude toward women pushed female slaves to the bottom rung of the ladder in the social order.

Dr. Flint's conduct toward Linda Brent verifies that Kemble's diary does not draw a counterfeit picture of how female slaves were influenced by their surroundings. His manners, while the slave is yet a girl, betray an impulse to have her accept that her best interest lies in submission "to his will in all things" (1973, 26). Around the slaveholder, "she is not allowed to have any pride of character" (29). Constantly referring to Linda as a body, "made for his use" (16), he sounds perfectly accustomed to raising slave girls to look at themselves as commodities whose worth comes from resting at his disposal. Dr. Flint swears that defying him amounts to "foolishly throwing away" (30) a sure shot at happiness. "Only let me arrange matters in my own way," he advises Linda. In return, he promises, "I would make a lady of you" (34).

Likewise, Ruth Hall's encounters with men in the wake of her husband's death bare a predilection among the males to situate women "at the lowest round of the ladder" (Fern [1855] 1997, 155). It is soon plain that their single design revolves around letting her exchange subjection for security. After Harry's funeral, Mr. Ellet and Dr. Hall, respectively, Ruth's father and father-in-law, talk about her as if she were a trifling thing, like a doll baby, for which one of them needs to look out. They decide to offer her help contingent upon her willingness to place her children in the custody of Dr. Hall. Since she rejects their bargain, they withdraw it. Ruth ends up starving and hounded by strangers who bet that she would be "so grateful for any little attention" and declare that she "may be bought with a yard of ribbon, or a [mere] breastpin" (88). With "every door of hope [seeming] shut," she is vexed by the prospect of earning a living in a local brothel where waves of "gray-haired men, business men, substantial-looking family men, and foppish-looking young men" give cash to "young and fair" or "wan and haggard" (112) females to satisfy their lusts.

It is reasonable to suspect that ideological, if not biological, mandates forced Antebellum women to create a culture distinct from the society at large for their self-fulfillment. The separate and unequal calibrations of men and women supply sufficient cause to guess that an identity alienated from the outside world harvested the grounds for a feminist community. As women's chances to find true happiness were held in contrast to men's opportunities, conceivably, one could presume that the lives of the former had to take on a psychology different from that of the latter. It would follow that their aesthetics would differ and that they would bring forth a literature of their own mapping aspirations and aversions antithetical to national traditions maintained by men. This line of reasoning started to gain sizable support in the 1970s.

Studies such as *The Female Imagination* (1975) by Patricia Meyer Spacks and also *A Literature of Their Own* (1977) by Elaine Showalter excited speculation that women have developed their own forms of writing that mirror the sensibility of a discrete feminine culture. Such analysis was advanced by critics in line with Helene Cixous and Julia Kristeva who ascribed to women unique signifying practices in literary discourse that they label *l'ecriture feminine*. In this respect, Carroll Smith-Rosenberg's essay "The Female World of Love and Ritual" (1975) was representative. It is also important to note the black female image recorded in Alice Walker's work "In Search of Our Mothers' Gardens" (1974), for it introduces the theory that black women have a literary heritage of their very own, gleaned from a singular social context, nurtured by a special sense, produced by a unique history. Walker's text specifically moved Barbara Smith to write "Toward a Black Feminist Criticism" (1977) and thereby to call for the institution of an analytical method qualified to tell how beautifully black women writers have captured the rites of an exclusive sorority.

A close reading though refutes any interpretation of *A Slave Girl* as an articulation of morals contrary to the nation's founding ideals. One occurrence in the tale, to be sure, certifies that the manuscript harmonizes with the acclaimed sentiments voiced by Patrick Henry on the eve of the American Revolution. It takes place during the earliest stage of Linda's escape from the grasp of Dr. Flint, nights before she resorts to hiding in her grandmother's garret for seven years. After a dreadful week "in terrible suspense," then, secretly, nursing a snake bite, gotten from hours spent "in a thicket of bushes" (Jacobs [1861] 1973, 100) to avoid trackers, Linda disregards messages from family members advising her "to return to [her] master, ask his forgiveness, and let him make an example of

[her]." She quickly notes, "When I started this hazardous undertaking, I had [willed] that, come what would, there should be no turning back." For a slogan, she embraces Henry's celebrated maxim "Give me liberty, or give me death" (101). Thus, she strictly spurns contrary counsel and stays on her chosen course.

Ruth Hall expresses a kindred brand of courage in reply to the denial of her brother Hyacinth, "the prosperous editor of the Irving Magazine," to open a door for her in publishing. A diehard chauvinist, he answered her plea in a letter, stating, "It is very evident that writing never can be *your* forte; you have no talent that way," (Fern [1855] 1997, 146) and instructing her, by implication, to pursue a typical female occupation involving housework. When the correspondence arrives, Ruth is at her wit's end. For want of bread to feed her two surviving daughters, she has had to release her oldest girl to her in-laws who hope to turn the child against her mother because they judge her flawed by an itch to find a livelihood outside traditional channels prescribed for her sex. Rather than forsake her ambition, on finishing her brother's retort, Ruth grins bitingly with a "hot tear" on her cheek. She concedes that it will take "a desperate struggle first," during which "*Pride* must sleep" (147), but, she vows, no matter how rocky or perilous the road might turn, she is going to put a twinkle in her girls' eyes by earning a decent living as a writer.

The frame of mind embodied in *Ruth Hall* never wants to overturn the initial grounds for the sustenance of American society; overall, it strives to rid them of an extraneous growth obscuring woman's rights in the land. It claims that a woman's natural strengths equal a man's in that each is born with a passion for liberty and a mind to savor it; so, men who feel superior to women are wrong. The foremost Fern scholar, Warren, argues, appropriately that the novel broadcasts "the promise of the American Dream." In other words, it serves as a statement in support of the country's most cherished code of conduct. Though, Warren admits, it works, in a Derridaean sense, as an unraveling of an absurdly rigid hierarchy serving men and seeing that "women [were] conditioned" to accept it as

a state "fixed by God and Nature," at any rate, the scholar
indicates that "it was a revolutionary book," not owing to a
design to slur the nation, but as a result of a scheme to dress
a woman in the manner of a public idol like Franklin for
the purpose of extracting a diametrical belief system,
embedded in the cultural matrix, barring women from
climbing "the ladder of success to fulfill the American
Dream." Associating *Ruth Hall* with *Ragged Dick* (1868)
the later work by Horatio Alger, she implicates that each
novel conjures up the same spirit. Warren professes that
Elizabeth Cady Stanton got it right, in saying, "The great
lesson taught in *Ruth Hall* is that God has given to woman
sufficient brain and muscle to work out her own destiny
unaided and alone."[4]

The soul at the heart of *A Slave Girl* impresses upon
the mind a related word to the wise. In personality, it
undermines a vital aspect of Estelle Jelinek's definition of
a typical autobiography by a woman as a style of discourse
that tends not to echo the sacred truths of its age. Frances
Smith Foster has divined that the slave narrative embodies
numerous "rhetorical strategies that are deliberate, though
subtle" ([1979] 1994, xxv) quizzes of "stereotypes and half-
truths" (xxiii). Her hunch holds water. Although Jacobs's
story explodes treasured myths about gender and race,
after all is said and done, the text does not signify a warrant to overthrow the country. As Joanne Braxton
acknowledges, *A Slave Girl* resonates with "the values
and language" (1989, 16) so dear to the freedom buffs who
forged the nation. Everything being equal, Walter Teller,
introducing the book, strikes a sound note by tagging it a
sample of "a genre of writing as distinctive to American
literature as the blues is to American music" (Jacobs [1861]
1973, ix).

With *Ruth Hall, A Slave Girl* endorses principles
that fall on American ears for all the world like hit tunes.
Each book stands, as may be expected, as a descendant to
Franklin's *Autobiography* as well as a close ancestor to

---

4. This summary is drawn from pages 130-42 in Warren's *Fanny Fern: An Independent
Woman* (New Brunswick, NJ: Rutgers University Press, 1992).

Alger's *Ragged Dick*. By the same token, they are related
to the stories of escape from slavery by Olaudah Equiano
and Frederick Douglass, on top of the sojourn at sea recollected by Richard Henry Dana. Within the context of
American culture, like the matching male manuscripts,
the women's writings are success stories with a thrilling
power. Sentiently, *Ruth Hall* and *A Slave Girl* picture
human potential in terms that stroke the national mind on
the subject.

Through her handling of Dr. Hall, Fern connotes
that Americans conceive, a person can cross from a poor,
old life to a rich, new one through an astute application of
learning in a fertile field of endeavor. She personifies her
husband's father as a person who is very proud of himself
because he has grown from being a poor boy in Vermont
toiling on a farm with "ploughs, hoes, and harrows" to a
gentleman in Massachusetts who has "managed to pick up
sufficient knowledge to establish himself" as a physician
whose practice is well known "as far as the next village"
(16). The author sheds a corresponding light on Ruth's
father. In complexion, she depicts Mr. Ellet as someone
who is "inordinately fond of talking" about how he has
come into the Bay State "a-foot, with a loaf of bread and a
sixpence, and now" owns real estate, and has "a nice little
sum stowed away in the bank for a rainy day" (158). Mr.
Ellet and Dr. Hall are a couple of "self-made men." A
comparable icon is John Walters. About the editor, who
gives Ruth her big break, Fern has her remember "having
heard Mr. Walter spoken of by somebody, at some time, as
a most energetic young man, who had wrung success from
an unwilling world, and fought his way, single-handed,
from obscurity to an honorable position in society, against,
what would have been to many, overwhelming odds" (185).
In unison, the three male figures hint at Fern's sense that a
faith in self-reliance has charmed the country and whetted
an appetite for tales about individual triumphs over hard
times that *Ruth Hall* has the ingredients to delight.

Figuratively, the elements mixed into Fern's novel
concoct a tantalizing flavor through a configuration of
Ruth that evokes her in the image of an untested swimmer

who, embarking from a bleak harbor, is tossed out of a
rickety vessel in a stormy sea and, devoid of help, treads
water until, with a resolve to pull through the disaster, she
tests her ability to stay afloat and, through steady efforts,
goes beyond all expectations. It is relevant that the book has
a reference to Daniel Defoe's trailblazing *Robinson Crusoe* (1719). *Ruth Hall* opens with the protagonist alone in
her bedroom at midnight, "gazing through" a small
window "upon the sparkling waters of the bay, glancing
and quivering 'neath the moon-beams" (3), and, plainly
unsettled beneath her father's roof, like young Crusoe,
Ruth presumably will be gratified by nothing save cutting
"a shining path through the waters" (8) and going to sea;
about to marry in the morning, she prays that matrimony
will grant her an "ark of refuge" from the world where
always "time, with its ceaseless changes, [rolls] on" (3).
Nonetheless, not long into the marriage, "wave after wave
of anguish [dash] over [her]" (49); a "gray dawn" (48)
delivers the maiden jolt through the demise of her first-
born daughter, Daisy, from illness; next, the typhus fever
seizes her husband and heaves him, "floating—drifting
sinking —soaring" (59), into the jaws of death. The two
events coupled with the refusal of family and friends to
come to her aid constrain Ruth to fend for herself or sink
into ruin. Fully seeing the world as a rocky climate from
which neither wedlock nor any institution or individual
can extend to a person a permanent shelter, she resorts to
looking to become a skillful enough writer to sustain herself, and with such direction, she soon calls to mind a
swimmer breasting "the billows, now rising high on the
topmost wave, now merged in the shadows, but still steer-
ing with straining sides," heading "for the nearing port of
Independence" (171). Like Crusoe alone in the world, Ruth
comes to determine in her mind that it is possible for her to
reap peace through her own pains, which she does by getting to be a prosperous columnist.

As Ruth manages to reach a latitude outlandish to
contemporary women, she projects that practical skills are
rather empowering. She poses that the fate of the average
woman is never to go far for want of a sensible education;

she is just prepared to act as a household item like a "parlor ornament" (166) or a "pliant tool" (205). Therefore, "for the common female employments and recreations," the writer urgently invites "unqualified disgust" (56) because they involve no more than a cheap chance to score by making "somebody's heart glad, —somebody's hearthstone bright" (6), to survive virtually by pleasing a man, in a world that daily wrecks anchors devised to hold a craft in place. Her inability to make ends meet from sewing manifests that women stood unfit to take care of themselves by reason of their inferior exposure to more lucrative public trades, such as business, medicine, or publishing, from which her father, Mr. Ellet, her father-in-law, Dr. Hall, and even her big brother, Hyacinth, have individually procured themselves a good life. While her single memory of her mother pertains to the way in which "she always looked uneasy about the time her father was expected home" (4), by turns, Ruth implies that women have long despaired from wrongly limited boundaries in the area of learning. The use of her writing skill gained in her girlhood to overcome her misfortune validates what Ruth portends.

The portrayal of Ruth says that licensing females to succeed in the fashion of the heroine is apt to promote the general welfare. As Ruth's writing career unfolds, she develops an audience whose lives her words inflame with hope. Her social impact is confirmed through a procession of letters from fans of her newspaper columns. A dying woman aware that the "earth recedes and eternity draws near" (174) addresses Ruth, writing under the pseudonym Floy, to let her know that her work, full of "sweet and soul-strengthening words" (175), has eased her suffering. To boot, a man writes a note to tell her, "I am a better son, a better brother, a better husband, and a better father, than I was before I [started] reading your articles" (235). Most importantly, Ruth's success guarantees women that the pursuit of a literary career will not direct them "out of their orbits," as holds Professor William Stearns, the self-described "genius" and master of Greek, Hebrew, and mathematics whose opinion evinces the current bias against women. The white heroine contradicts Stearns's insistence "that the *female* mind is incapable of producing anything which may be strictly termed *literature*" (214). By then following those allegations with the examination of Ruth's head by the pseudoscientific phrenologist named Professor Finman, who finds the protagonist intelligent and tells her that her "whole character . . . arises from the influence of [her] education" (219), Fern intimates that the "quack" is really a "sage" and the "sage" a "quack," proving that the conventional image of the feminine gender is off-base, and so the writer urges members of her sex to search for self-fulfillment in pursuits out of the ordinary for them.

With a matching consciousness of the local taste for yarns about folks who pull off the trick of rising above their original station in life through their own initiative, Jacobs brewed her book in compliance with the recipe that spiced *Ruth Hall*. In *A Slave Girl*, Linda's memories of her father and grandmother attribute to them the kind of human traits that fascinated Americans. She describes her father as someone who was a slave in name only, because, through a mastery of carpentry, he has found a means of "supporting himself," of managing "his own affairs," and of making himself a "comfortable home" ([1861] 1973, 3), in which to protect his daughter and son from a host of horrors swirling in the surrounding society sustained by the public practice of black slavery. Linda remembers her grandmother's winning control of her life in the same manner after a difficult youth. The narrator reminisces:

> I have often heard her tell how hard she fared
> during childhood. But as she grew older she
> evinced so much intelligence, and was so faith-
> ful, that her master and mistress could not
> help seeing it was for their interest to take
> care of [her]. She became an indispensable per-
> sonage in the household, officiating in all
> capacities. . . . She was much praised for her
> cooking; and her nice crackers became so
> famous in the neighborhood that many people
> were desirous of obtaining them. [Thus], she
> asked permission of her mistress to bake crack-
> ers at night, after all the housework was done;

> and she obtained leave to do it. . . . The busi-
> ness proved profitable; and each year she laid
> by a little, which was saved for a fund to pur-
> chase her children. (3-4)

Aunt Martha, her maternal grandmother, like her father, "considered so intelligent and skillful in his trade" (3), has a familiar ring. Linda attributes to the woman and the man an entrepreneurial energy fortified by intelligence and focused on independence that measures up well to the enterprising drive that delivered unto "Founding Father" Franklin fame and fortune.

Of course, Jacobs's portrait of Linda rendered her deserving of the title "self-made woman" and so appealing to the national palate. Linda calls to mind a vision of life as a golden adventure that can be as wonderful as "fairly sailing on the Chesapeake Bay" with the sun in one's face and the wind at one's back, realizing "what grand things air and sunlight are" (163), following a fresh flight from a murky swamp, swarming with toxic snakes. Her story ranges from slavery to freedom. It paints human bondage as a state similar to being stranded in a marsh through its passages about Linda's "wretched night" in Snaky Swamp spent beating off serpents stealing ceaselessly around her. The portrait's point about slavery leaks out, when Linda comments, "But even those large, venomous snakes were less dreadful to my imagination than the white men [i.e., slaveholders] in that community called civilized" (116). Later, freedom strikes her as an "inestimable boon" (206) that places her in a pleasant position to entertain, instead of "gloomy recollections," uplifting ideas, coloring her mind with notions "like light, fleecy clouds floating over a dark and troubled sea" (208). Be it true or false, such a narration was bound to move a national audience.

Linda's progress touts spreading knowledge. The character's advancement pivots on the training of her mind. She comes to look lucky to have learned, as a girl, first of all, never ever to dream that she "was a piece of merchandise, [entrusted] to [others] for safe keeping, and liable to be demanded of them at any moment" (3), and, second, how "to read and spell" (6) words put on paper.

Linda conveys human reason as a property able to yield
rotten and rosy results, contingent upon its breeding. Her
ordeal tells that exposure to enslavement, unmitigated,
degenerates the intellect; what the black character goes
through provokes her to testify that slavery engenders a
savage mentality that arouses impetuous conduct in every
member of the system; the practice "is a curse to the whites
as well as to the blacks." In truth, she remarks, "It makes
the white fathers cruel and sensual, [while it renders] the
sons violent and licentious; it contaminates the daughters,
and makes the wives wretched" (53). Speaking of enslaved
black men, she identifies slavery as a very severe form of
miseducation:

> Some poor creatures have been so brutalized
> by the lash that they will sneak out of the
> way to give their masters free access to their
> wives and daughters. Do you think this proves
> the black man to belong to an inferior order of
> beings? What would *you* be, if you had been
> born and brought up a slave, with generations
> of slaves for ancestors? I admit that the black
> man *is* inferior. But what is it that makes him
> so? It is the ignorance in which the white men
> compel him to live; it is the torturing whip
> that lashes manhood out of him; it is the fierce
> bloodhounds of the south . . . *They* do the
> work. (43-44)

Afterward, you can respect her musing, "Lives that flash
in sunshine, and lives that are born in tears, receive their
hue from circumstances" (61); also, you can comprehend
how learning to suppose that she was never meant to live
for the good of others gives her the nerve to resist Dr. Flint
and that having at her disposal expertise in literacy read-
ies her to dupe him, by post, into believing that she has
slipped beyond his reach when, in fact, she is hiding a
stone's throw away.

The incidents moving from slavery to freedom in
A Slave Girl, tell that the common slave's upbringing ten-
dered knowledge "sufficient for a slave's condition" (172).
Had she realized it alone, she never would have sum-

moned the strength and skill to escape slavery, elude capture, and evade corruption, she never would have told her
tale, and she never would have contributed to domestic
tranquility. The episodes of Linda's story climax upon her
awkward arrival at the "wood wharf in Philadelphia."
When she buys some "double veils and gloves" (164) in a
local shop and fails to understand the prices for them, she
reminds the reader of Franklin's marveling at the value
of "three great Puffy Rolls" on the day of his clumsy landing in the city. It is fitting that the narrator compares herself to Robinson Crusoe earlier during her exile in the roof
of her grandmother's house. By the time that Linda arrives
in the City of Brotherly Love she has gone from being akin
to a shipwrecked sailor washed ashore, spooked, on an
alien isle to resembling a ready builder with tools handy to
make herself at home in the world. Her transformation
deposits that people resemble plants; they depend foremost
on their breeding. *A Slave Girl*, in effect, performed a public service; though, on the surface, it might have seemed
just meant "to kindle a flame of compassion in [local]
hearts for [Linda's] sisters who [were] still in bondage, suffering as [she had herself] once suffered" (28), subliminal-
ly, at least, it put the country in mind of the logic that had
breathed life into the land.

A *Slave Girl* lends credence to the Quaker tenet that
humans are endowed with an "inner light" to shine in the
world. The book jibes with Plato's notion that humans at
birth possess a personal potential awaiting refinement to
rear them into just republicans. Most of all, it relates the
national belief that people have a natural right to map their
own way in the world because they have a power, once prepared, to chart a sound course for themselves. Again, the
theme aligns the slave narrative with Fern's novel. The
motif of *Ruth Hall*, along with that of *A Slave Girl*, solicits
universal suffrage; in each, it is imagined that people
have a capacity to care for themselves that makes them
worthy of independence in the wake of instruction. Jacobs
with Fern had many counterparts.

As Jane Roland Martin observes in regard to Mary
Wollstonecraft's provocative *Vindication of the Rights of*

Woman (1792), the writings at issue by the black and white women belong to "the same powerful intellectual tradition as the American Declaration of Independence" (Martin 1985, 76) advanced by maverick thinkers like Locke who proclaimed that "men" are reasonable creatures for whom education forms a key element in their endeavors to achieve fruition. *A Slave Girl*, in alliance with *Ruth Hall*, reflects a channel in a stream of consciousness restricted to the subterranean burrows of an underground movement ever since social orders demanding conformity to moor the status quo surfaced with designs to make women bashful servants devoted to bossy men. The tales of the American women tacitly join the Wollstonecraft work, an outrage to her native England, in an attack on the broad frame of mind that threatened to confine their gender to seeking satisfaction by learning to be comparable a doll manufactured to comfort the masculine side of humanity, which deportment Jean-Jacques Rousseau advocated in his construction of femininity throughout *Emile* ([1762] 1979), where the Frenchman figures:

> Thus the whole education of women ought to
> relate to men. To please men, to be useful to
> them, to make herself loved and honored by
> them, to raise them when young, to care for
> them when grown, to counsel them, to console
> them, to make their lives agreeable and sweet;
> these are the duties of women at all times, and
> they ought to be taught from childhood. (365)

Martin affirms that "*A Vindication of the Rights of Woman* represents one long rejection of Rousseau's definition of [a woman], the education he would give her, and the person he would have her become" (Martin 71). Wollstonecraft's book shows that she wanted to challenge how the Frenchman looked at her sex; she specifies that his image of women was "grossly unnatural" (Wollstonecraft [1792] 1975, 107), seeing, he sensed, "a woman should never for a moment feel independent," *parce que*, he had been taught to suspect, "with respect to the female character, obedience is the grand lesson which ought to be impressed with unrelenting rigour" (108); opening her publication with remorse "that the civilization which has hitherto taken place in the world has been very partial" toward the formulation of demanding men and deceitful women by means of "a false system of education" that is "more anxious" to turn the membership of the feminine gender into packs of "alluring mistresses than affectionate wives and rational mothers," yet is geared up to let men "exact respect" (79) through their own initiative enabled by a chance "to unfold their faculties" (81); hence, for centuries across the globe, communities have subjected women to being judged inferior to men and the regard has bedeviled everyone by provoking men to be overbearing and women obsequious. Fern concurred with the English writer's opinion about the customary breeding of men when she had her fabrication, Ruth, remark about her sibling: "The world smiled on her brother Hyacinth. He was handsome, and gifted. He could win fame, and what was better, love (Fern 4). Furthermore, Jacobs echoed Wollstonecraft by having her persona Linda confess in the aftermath of her stealing away to the North:

> I like a straightforward course, and am always reluctant to resort to subterfuges. So far as my ways have been crooked, I charge them all upon slavery. It was that system of violence and wrong which left me no alternative but to enact a falsehood. (171)

The bottom line is that all three female authors mentioned saw women as rational beings, as much as mortals of the masculine gender, who can and should be educated to gain autonomy.

Across the Atlantic over 3000 miles southwest of London the intellectual tradition to which Fern and Jacobs would belong by the mid-nineteenth century gained a member in Abigail Adams during the Enlightenment that witnessed the appearance of Wollstonecraft's *Vindication.* One can never pinpoint the source of the philosophical body's drift. It is conceivable that from the hour men undertook to dominate women in social orders on the planet, some of their would-be subordinates nobly resisted their concerted efforts. Murasaki Shikibu's *Genji monogatari* (c.1008), the classic Japanese narrative customarily considered the world's first novel, assures, by the early light of the eleventh century, that women were conscious and clever enough to craft a splendid montage of social manners. *L'Epistre au Dieu d'amours* written by Christine de Pizan in 1399, certifies that the gender harbored an appreciable antipathy, in the midst of the European Renaissance, for caricatures of females as flowers indebted to men for bringing worth, like sunlight, to otherwise unproductive lives. There is nothing in history to suggest that Adams broke new ground by telling her husband that men needed, in relation to women, to abdicate "the harsh title of Master for the more tender and endearing one of Friend," so that, instead of seeing women as "vassals" (Rossi 1988, 11), they would behave toward them as equals. The known facts assert that she did not establish a precedent on American soil; intellectuals like Anne Bradstreet preceded her, and Frances Wright, who trusted that "liberty and knowledge ever go hand in hand" (Rossi 100), soon succeeded her, in advance of Sarah Grimke, Margaret Fuller, and Elizabeth Cady Stanton, discerning that males, by custom, have denied females an adequate education and, in the process, demeaned and disparaged them without cause.

Among women in early American society pushing to upgrade the training of their sex, Jacobs never was the sole black in the movement. *The Memoirs of Elleanor Eldridge* (1838) about the commercial success achieved by the black female subject conveys the respect for women that would be expressed in *A Slave Girl*. Moving orators, like Jarena Lee, Sojourner Truth, and Frances Harper, delivered speeches in public urging universal suffrage in the nineteenth century. On September 21, 1832, Maria W. Stewart gave a lecture at Franklin Hall in Boston, which made her the first native woman to take a political stand in front of a sexually mixed crowd. In general, regarding blacks, Stewart observed that they "feel a common desire to rise above the condition of servants and drudges" (Porter 137); very certain that black women could realize the wish, she solicited a nod from her "fairer sisters" by inquiring of them, "Had we had the opportunity that you have had, to improve our moral and mental faculties, what would have hindered our intellects from being as bright, and our manners from being as dignified as yours?" (Porter 138). Stewart's perspective received backing from the thematic thrust slanting *Behind the Scenes* (1868), Elizabeth Keckley's story tracing her climb from the lowly existence of a slave in Virginia to the lofty position of a dressmaker in the Lincoln White House. In actuality, untold African American women, like Jacobs, believed that females of every complexion could benefit themselves and society, if they were raised to do more than oblige others. The most concise expression of their outlook appeared as a letter from an author identified as Matilda in an 1827 edition of the pioneering black newspaper *Freedom's Journal*, published in New York by Samuel Cornish and John Russwurm; she argued that black female schooling should feature much more than "mathematical knowledge" that is "limited to 'fathoming the dish-kettle,'" with "enough of history" to know "that our grandfather's father lived and died," for we are made for more than housekeeping, we "have minds . . . capable and deserving of culture," and, though "we possess not the advantages with those of our sex, whose skins are not coloured," if properly instructed, we could be "up and doing" well (Aptheker 1951, 89) wonderful deeds and works.

"Matilda" may well have been the pen name for an educated woman, like Sarah Forten, the Philadelphia sailmaking mogul James Forten's daughter, who printed political letters under aliases. The use of a nom de plume was a routine procedure among female authors opposed to traditional sex roles ordering masculine supremacy. They had to mask their true identities to avoid censure. Open resistance to custom in writing was seriously asking for trouble. Whether black or white, by putting her thoughts on paper for public recognition, a woman was sure to raise eyebrows; meanwhile, by pitching social criticism into the deal, she was bound to stir a storm of protest condemning the author for indulging in an off-color exercise. Jacobs knew, it was unwise for a woman to make her person and plans plain in print on any occasion, but particularly in instances that posed glaring challenges to male prerogatives. "Woman can whisper" her complaints, Jacobs wrote Amy Post, "into the ear of a very dear friend" with more ease "than she can record them for the world to read" (Yellin 242) in order to win sympathy.

In a study covering American autobiography, the works of Jacobs and Fern belong side by side. Pressure to produce their stories under an assumed name affected both of their compositions. In her groundbreaking Introduction to *Ruth Hall*, Warren reminds the reader that in the middle of the nineteenth century, "it was not considered proper for a woman to write about herself" (1986, xxxiv). The social attitude compelled Sara Payson Willis to write masked as Fanny Fern to deflect public criticism; it also incited the author to have her fictional character, Ruth Hall, disguise her real self through the technique of the pseudonym "Floy" to dodge harsh public raps, "some maintaining her to be a man" (Fern 170), a number dubbing her a spinster, swindler, or screwball, and a bunch manifesting chagrin at the thought of her penning social commentary. In order not to seem like individuals acting out of character, Fern and Jacobs wrote truthfully about their lives by appearing not to do so. *Ruth Hall* and *A Slave Girl* carry imprints of fiction. The novel recounts Fern's own history of becoming a widow and scrambling to propel herself and her children to better seasons despite rotten treatment from her relatives; names in the book are fake versions of real ones, and events are doctored editions of actual ones resulting from an effort to make the story seem made up, but, in essence, it is Fern's personal narrative of how she climbed out of disaster and deprivation to fame and fortune. Although Jacobs prefaces her tale by stating, "Reader, be assured this narrative is no fiction," it is not "nevertheless, strictly true" (Jacobs xiii); it blurs the line between fact and myth; the protagonist in *A Slave Girl*, Linda Brent, is an alter ego, not the author herself, and on top of the rest of the character names being fictitious, a recent study completed by Yellin,[5] comparing *A True Tale of Slavery* (1861), a newly recovered story from Jacobs's real brother John, to *A Slave Girl*, leads to the conclusion that the black female author stretched the truth in many ways to render her life as a symbol of how a woman could rise by her own efforts in society. John Blassingame's skepticism about the veracity of *A Slave Girl*, related in his groundbreaking investigation entitled *The Slave Community*, becomes understandable; with Fern, Jacobs constructed an autobiography arrayed in the accoutrements of a novel.

Apparently plain and simple, yet rather profound, *A Slave Girl* and *Ruth Hall* could fairly be mistaken for a couple of sentimental fictions from two of the nineteenth-century writers whom Nathaniel Hawthorne termed "a damned mob of scribbling women" (1910, 75) so eager "to make a show of their hearts" (30). Nina Baym defined the literary genre as the "woman's novel." Using the form, the scholar explained, hundreds of women told "with variations, a single tale" about "a young girl who is deprived of the supports she had rightly or wrongly depended [upon] to sustain her throughout life and is faced with the necessity of winning her own way in the world," and the story ends with "happy marriages," which (in the last century) made it a simulation of the "successful accomplishment" of "the formation and assertion of a feminine ego" (1978, 11-12) with a soft side for domesticity. The narrative appeared "in two parallel versions." Baym noted:

> In one, the heroine begins as a poor and friendless child. Most frequently an orphan, she sometimes only thinks herself to be one, or has by necessity been separated from her parents for an infinite time. In the second, the heroine is a pampered heiress who becomes

---

5. In "Through Her Brother's Eyes" which appears in *Harriet Jacobs and Incidents in the Life of a Slave Girl*, (New York: Cambridge University Press, 1996), edited by Deborah Garfield and Rafia Zafar, Yellin shows that *A True Tale of Slavery* presents "a different perspective . . . on the people, places, and events Harriet Jacobs wrote about" (45).

> poor and friendless in midadolescence, through
> the death or financial failure of her legal pro-
> tectors. (35)

Unquestionably, Jacobs's slave narrative resembles the
first version of the "woman's novel." Fern's fiction favors
the second arrangement.

Regardless, the white and black women's writings
deviate from the established convention. Hawthorne noted
the difference in *Ruth Hall*. He admitted that he "enjoyed
it a good deal," for it managed to "throw off the restraints of
decency" that caused women to write "like emasculated
men" who as a rule were "only to be distinguished from
male authors by greater feebleness and folly" (1910, 76-78).
Hawthorne fully sensed that Fern meant to do more with
her novel than reinforce the outrageous expectations for
women. Thematically, her novel and *A Slave Girl* have
more in common with *Allen Lucas, the Self-Made Man*
(1847) by Emily Chubbuck Judson than *The Wide, Wide
World* (1850) by Susan Warner or *The Lamplighter* (1854)
by Maria Cummins, which teaches women to treasure submission and is a close cousin to *Jane Eyre* (1847). The
denouements in the books from Fern and Jacobs validate
their discrete motifs. Marriage is the key to happiness for
neither Ruth nor Linda; the first begins with marriage
and ends with widowhood; the second opens with seduction
and closes with celibacy. In each, money, not marriage,
brings peace. Instead of finishing with marriage licenses
materializing as certificates of success, *Ruth Hall* offers a
bank statement of the protagonist's worth, and *A Slave Girl*
volunteers a bill of sale for Linda's freedom to signal her
triumph over social frustration.

The outcomes in the novel and the slave narrative
underscore the social significance born in the texts. *Ruth
Hall* and *A Slave Girl* valorize a common way of talking
about the human condition that has fixed the parameters
for the cultural mainstream. An inclination to perceive
females simply as a world of difference from the universe
of males, signifying normatively the summit of reason,
forced Fern with Jacobs to recall her life in public from

behind a mask and leave the audience to miss its resonant expression of the social ethos upheld in the famous personal narratives published by Equiano and Franklin as well as those issued by Douglass and Dana. In the most frank autobiography, a bit of fiction is involved; to tell the truth, the whole truth, and nothing but the truth in writing about one's life would take a very precise memory, and the end result would be a mundane chronicle of events with neither rhyme nor reason. Jacobs and Fern avoided such a trite consequence. They fictionalized above average amounts of the facts about their lives in their accounts. Their labors add up to American autobiographies, for they are life stories recounted by their subjects in a national style conveying an epic theme.

By the end of their narratives, there is no urgency to conclude that they are indistinguishable from brotherly male texts. A shade of difference in their tones parts the first volume from the second one. In both cases, carefully set words exhibit a design to urge unchaining folks from custom to let them enjoy the best of all possible worlds by cultivating fields of freedom through the use of learning. The female texts voice a broader, more democratic sense of "men" and lay a greater emphasis on community. As Braxton digests, about autobiographies by black women, a communal sense absent from the men's self disclosures pervades the books by Jacobs and Fern, disallowing that any human is innately superior to anyone else. It is most evident in the women's concern for their children, whom they prize as living appendages to themselves or, as Jacobs implies, vines extending out of their hearts. There is a dedication to freedom for blacks and whites, males and females, young and old, everyone without exception in the women's material, which is muted by a fidelity to traditional male privileges in the men's products. A *Slave Girl* like *Ruth Hall* stirs one to note that it praises the American Dream with a pure pitch striking deep by means of a specific accent; in the country, with its mate, it has the ring of a bittersweet song for liberty from taxing customs.

5

Territorial Waters

Lifting as We Climb
— *Motto of the National Association of Colored Women*

Seas run deep and shallow. Social causes much fare the same. In point of fact, every culture rests on principles that sway the majority and others that stir only miscellaneous minorities. The goals pooling the most striking accord mesh and muster a system of belief, a mode of outlook, or a frame of reference that launches and routes a society. In lieu of such, an attempt to sustain a working culture would have as good a shot at success as a mission to sail a ship over the Seven Seas with a crew of sailors all speaking in disparate tongues. The United States is a model case. An evolving social order, it has risen and run from a catholic perspective overarching myriad parochial leanings like a living language hosting sundry dialects. A broad survey of distinguished American autobiographies written over the last few centuries clarifies the matter.

An innovative literary practice has taken root in the land. It involves "personal expressions of the meaning of life" (Sayre 1981, 13) in the form of a story commemorating a writer's private history through a motif speaking of the world as a big sea, a site where constant change occurs, a situation in which a heroic figure is bound to favor a bold swimmer. In brief, the land has nurtured the growth of a new epic form reflective of a binding cultural subjectivity about humanity reading people as creatures equipped to enjoy liberty through the use of learning. It is a convention gathered from a heritage seeded by creations like the *Confessions of St. Augustine* (c.400) and also *Don Quixote* (1605), in addition to *Robinson Crusoe* (1719). Still, its flowers have blossomed with the disposition of a hybrid breed sown by the domestic climate.

More exactly, a species of autobiography has arisen in the country acting as an inscription of a widespread faith in the application of useful knowledge for the general welfare. Studying the literary trend prompted Robert Sayre to write thoughtfully that "autobiographies, in all their bewildering number and variety, offer the student in American Studies a broader and more direct contact with American experience than any other kind of writing" (11). He fathomed that a variety of citizens have recollected their lives in narratives constructed to convey and celebrate the social ethos behind a sense of heroism widespread within the territorial borders of the national development since the eighteenth century. His argument held water. If one collects a random sample of the writing in question, including specimens from early to recent epochs in the country's history, one will discover evidence of an autobiographical convention with the status of a new experiment in world literature practiced by a sea of diverse American individuals.

Regarding works in the tradition, Sayre argued that "the most uniquely American, we now see, was the slave narrative, created *sui generis* by the conditions of a racially and politically divided country" (22). Again, he had a point. Scholars have cited Franklin's written, self history as the prototype for a convention of autobiography that bares the American soul. They have underestimated the standing of slave narratives like the books by Equiano, Douglass, and Jacobs. These black life stories have gone inadequately appreciated, for recurring criticism has disseminated the conviction that the complexion (if not "race") of their creators created a critical difference in the character of their writings locating them in significance beyond the bounds of the cultural mainstream. Richard Gilman invited that kind of thinking through his book *The Confusion of Realms* (1969) where he perceives African American autobiographies as little more than exotic myths for blacks, and blacks alone, to live by. The vision misses the ironic way in which slavery groomed black people for the role of a priestly caste ordained to remind members of their congregation to keep the faith. Margaret Just Butcher claimed that bondage planted black Americans "deep in the subsoil of American life" (1972, 10), where they landed "a significant and symbolic position at the center of America's struggle for the full [growth] of the tradition of freedom" (18); her reasoning supports the conclusion that circumstances have set blacks up to have their life stories stand as epic tales without the slightest cause to rate them below the *Autobiography* in the annuals of the country's literary history accounts.

Superstition and hypocrisy have placed the African American in a position to be viewed in American society as either a resident alien or a domestic medicine man prone to revere countercultural feelings and thus unlikely to observe a moral compass pointing in a direction treasured by true Americans. Equating African Americans with foreign transients committed to a polar code of conduct has circulated in the culture since before Thomas Jefferson in *Notes on the State of Virginia* (1785) matched blacks with orangutans living lives governed by passion rather than thought. Winthrop Jordan has located the idea's origins at the start of the country's gestation decades prior to Jefferson's birth. Even though different scholars have dated it otherwise, Equiano's autobiography does, if nothing else, establish that it was washing over the country on the eve of the Revolutionary War. James Baldwin's "Stranger in the Village" demonstrates that it has ebbed and flowed into the twentieth century. The notion hangs on an awful fallacy which assumes that during ancient history, while agrarian white clans, directed by intuition, were absorbed in tasks leading to the erection of the monuments that would mark Western civilization, nomadic black tribes, driven by instinct, went roaming through dark jungles, expending their raw energies on hunting and gathering exploits devoid of lasting results. Inadvertently, Baldwin's essay avows, aids, and abets the illusion by comparing his stay alone in a Swiss hamlet to a mode of estrangement that captures the black experience in American society; about the villagers and himself, he says:

> The most illiterate among them is related, in a way that I am not, to [artists like] Dante, Shakespeare, Michelangelo, Aeschylus, Da Vinci, Rembrandt, and Racine; the cathedral at Chartres [expresses] something to them which it cannot say to me, as indeed would New York's Empire State Building. . . . Out of their hymns and dances come Beethoven and Bach. Go back a few centuries and they are in their full glory—but I am in Africa, watching the conquerors arrive. (1983, 165)

The painted picture leaves only ample room for imagining Americans of African ancestry merely as descendants to unreflective kin planting them against the main currents of social thought in the nation.

The evaluation of blacks has soothed consciences. Early America mandated a concept of white supremacy to mask maddening paradoxes. First of all, the main reading of humanity promised all "men" that they are born with a capacity to elevate themselves. However, since everyone could become uplifted, how could anyone feel distinct in the world when other "men" could rise up, too? Someone had to remain situated on the bottom rung of the social ladder to render individual progress measurable. Second, the communal frame of mind involved a trust that "men" are made for liberty; so, how could the practice of keeping blacks enslaved be warranted? Meanwhile, how much could the country grow without cheap labor? For slavery to exist in the social order, the slaves needed to amount to "not men." Blacks were drafted to fill the bill; they were perceived as bodies akin to beasts of burden, ranking about three-fifths of whites in worth, born with nothing to gain from learning, for want of reason, and the vision eclipsed the paradoxes that haunted the community.

Under the influence of the racist regard for blacks, well-meaning whites have sought to improve black social standing by portraying them as manifestations of a "noble savage." A flock of abolitionists, such as Harriet Beecher Stowe, clung to the appraisal and likened black people to children who take life in stride, instead of wrestling with it in the fashion of civilized men bent on subjecting it to their will. Whites overly intellectualize everything, the disposition has implied; they would be far better off if they mimicked the artless conduct inherited by black people. Norman Mailer revivified the suspicion in "The White Negro," where, in 1950s slang, he professes that whites are square and will never be hip until they dig the crazy way that black cats let it all hang out and play it cool the whole time. The notion would have black folks set on pedestals like statues sculpted to counsel citizens to give free rein to their instincts.

Neither science nor history bids seeing African stock different in constitution from European progeny to a degree disinclining or disabling the former from relating to the country's pioneer spirit dedicated to the proposition that people are born with a right and a reason to chart their own courses in life. Pro-slavery ideologues insisted that blacks in America would drift like flotsam at sea if released from bondage, because their blood turned them into capricious mental midgets in proportion to whites. Since slavery days, however, American medical science, advanced by Charles Drew, has proven that plasma is a lubricant, like motor oil, with little influence, if any, on human worth. W.E.B. Du Bois detected in "the thought of the older South,—the sincere and passionate belief that somewhere between men and cattle, God created a *tertium quid*, and called it a Negro," a funny, foolish fellow, (1996, 146) possibly very amiable but trivial. The scholar located nothing in the scientific data banks of his time to approve racial thinking, besides "the grosser physical differences of color, hair, and bone" (40). Today biologists express certainty that people come from a mixture of genes drawn from pools retaining a quantity of distinctive traits. They add that more genetic variety tends to appear among classes of pools than it does between any two groups. Only apologists for racism in line with William Shockley and Arthur Jensen still argue that biological traits divide whites and blacks into diametric species of greater and lesser weight. The available evidence confirms that both groups came to America with the good sense to realize the country's promise.

Blacks arrived on the coast that would become the nation's eastern shoreline in the same way as most white immigrants. They were either explorers or servants. After black Pedro Alonzo Nino navigated the *Santa Maria* to the New World for Christopher Columbus, in 1538 a Spaniard of African descent named Estevanico, "Little Stephen," directed an expedition that opened a passage to Spanish settlements in the future territory of New Mexico and Arizona. Eight years earlier, Africans exploring with Lucas Vasquez de Ayllon settled in what would come to be the state of South Carolina and became the original non-Native Americans to organize a community in the Northwestern Hemisphere. In 1619, more Africans called Pedro, Antoney, and Isabella disembarked from an armed mysterious Dutch vessel at Jamestown with two other black women and fifteen men. Lerone Bennett has recorded that they came ashore, like "many, perhaps most, of the first whites," as indentured servants permitted to gain property and freedom through an interval of contractual labor for wealthy planters. For "a period of forty years or more, [these] black settlers accumulated land, voted, testified in court and mingled with whites on a basis of equality" ([1962] 1984, 35). Unfortunately, people shifting in and out of indentured servitude rendered the workforce unstable; knowing it and wanting to secure the economy, the South began turning the tide on blacks in the 1660s; the region passed a flood of laws restricting them to slavery for life.

The legal changes sanctioned looking at blacks as exceptions to the rule in the country. Historically, African American ancestry never justified the treatment; they never wandered through an era without sustaining a logical order; they proved thoughtful enough to fend for themselves. In every millennium, black people exhibited the wherewithal to build empires in the Old World. They conceived Egypt up the Nile in the continent's eastern region long before the Greeks had a chance to forge their mythology; through the labors of black natives, Carthage arose to prominence along the Mediterranean Sea prior to Rome's brilliant ascent; and West African blacks produced Ghana, Mali, and Songhay which developed into global centers of learning and trade around the city of Timbuktu, the site of the University of Sankore, during the Dark Ages, when whites in Europe languished in isolation from world affairs. In all honesty, the rise and fall of empires have punctuated the history of whites as well as blacks. Of course, in most cases, the elders of black folks dwelled in pious, productive, agrarian areas comparable to Equiano's birthplace. But how unlike were they from Franklin's ancestral village in Ecton? Outside each, a sovereignty seated in a capital like London monopolized knowledge and power; the majority of the local masses consisted of illiterate peasants who lived off the land in rural settings with tools made by hand.

The historical record establishes that the black and white diaspora absorbed into the nation came from parallel backgrounds. It illustrates that blacks and whites from near as well as far have displayed ingenuity in specific manners, demonstrating that human behavior is learned, not inborn. Training deserves blame or credit for human conduct. An infant of any descent who dwells from birth in a French household will speak like the rest of the house by three years of age. As Jacques Barzun has seen, none of humanity possesses traits "immutable and determinant within the shifting frame of time and environment" (1937, 124). Social climates set the stage for human action.

Erstwhile in the 16th century, when Islam reigned in Songhay, Ahmed Baba, "the last chancellor of the University of Sankore," wrote forty books in Arabic and boasted "one of richest libraries of his day," containing nearly 2000 volumes (Clark 1986, 633). He existed as a product of his place and did no more than other blacks did in other sections of the world. Elsewhere, for example, during the peak of imperial Rome, Terence of Carthage, a boy carted to the European city as booty to slave for his captor, developed a mastery of Latin en route to scripting comic plays that would lay the foundation for the modern comedy of manners. Moreover, Aleksandr Pushkin, scion to Abyssinians on his mother's side, early in the the 19th century caught Slavic speech with sufficient skill to put pen to paper and produce prototypes of Russian poetry. Descended from black Haitians, Alexandre Dumas grew amply fluent in French to take Paris by storm with a torrent of tales about chivalry such as *Le Comte de Monte-Cristo* (1845). It is also noteworthy that the Numidian Aurelius Augustinus, known as well as St. Augustine, who frittered away his youth drifting around the northern and southern shores of the Mediterranean (while Christianity expanded, and Rome collapsed), matured into an expert rhetorician, formulated a paradigm for Catholicism in *The City of God* (426), and devised in his *Confessions* the initial autobiographical manuscript in Western memory. Every feat works to show that black ancestry bequeathed them a legacy of achievement in extensive situations.[1]

By the eighteenth century, one could have logically supposed that a child of Benin, like Equiano, hauled to the New World as a black slave for the good of whites, was bound to learn the local way of talking about human nature

---

1. During the last 500 years, historians in Western civilization have grown accustomed to assuming that any one who ever did anything noteworthy in the culture was white. Hence, St. Augustine has been considered *white* along with Terence. The race of Dumas and Pushkin has gone unspoken or presumed white. Yet, all of these authors had to be black according to the criterion for racial categorization established in the South close to 300 years ago which says that every one with *black* ancestry is black. By that standard, the given writers were either black or light blacks because they either had an unmixed or mixed black heritage. They had to have black ancestry because they had ancestors from Africa and Africa has always been dominated by blacks and light blacks. It is highly unlikely that any of the authors under consideration would look like foreigners today in *Upper* Egypt, the *cradle* of Western civilization, where the population favors African Americans in coloring. For further discussion, see footnote #1 in "Blackwall Hitch," in addition to #8 and #9 in "Crow's Nest." A book mentioned in an earlier footnote, *The World's Great Men of Color* (Macmillan, 1967) by J. A. Rogers, is especially worth considering.

and shout it from the mountaintops. Blacks like him had already managed such exploits in plenty of places. Also, one could have guessed that blacks never knew a greater motive to seek those sorts of triumphs other than their travails in the grim bowels of bondage, where dreams of rising in stature came daily to haunt waking hours. At the sound of people calling freedom a natural right, Equiano pricked up his ears. Sailing around the New World as ordered by the Philadelphia Quaker Robert King, Equiano acquired a broad exposure to the social ethos and deemed it to his liking. He realized that the residents shared a sense of division from Old World traditions stifling expression; they saw themselves as participants in a great awakening meant to increase creativity for generations to come by releasing people to reach their full potential through the use of learning; more importantly, they judged the practice of enslaving "men" indecent. How could he not have cried, Amen to all that? His *African* tells you that he attended and approved American discourse well enough to forge a prototype for a literary convention upholding the outlook behind the nation.

As reported earlier, within the moral borders of the mainstream, an underground stream of consciousness surfaced during the eighteenth century. Run from place after place, since the emergence of human societies, for raising choice above custom, the thinking at issue sees all "men" born equal to the extent that they are endowed with rationality entitling them to manage their own affairs free of coercion. Prior civilizations spawned mighty empires sanctioned by visions of the cosmos as a battlefield in which men and women came into being with predestined duties to meet specific fates. The outlook backed emperors across Africa, Asia, and Europe, dubbed pharaoh, sheik, and king, among other royal titles. The average person dwelled in a tribe, if not a clan, that expected its members to frown on personal ambition. People grew to accept that they were meant to maintain the station into which they were born; under the circumstances, the idea of seeking to reform one's status was deemed barbarous. Social orders took on the air of a ship manned by rowers commanded by a captain, assisted by mates. Everyone was bound by a tradition that posted ordinary horizons near the level of chattel.

As indicated at the start of this study, epic poems glorified the dominant social consciousness that supported earlier society. They maintained that forces beyond one's control have him at their mercy. For his good, they warned, he should practice piety to appease the powers that be. It is impossible to cheat fate. One should never doubt that he was born where he belonged. To find peace, he should keep up the grounds of his ancestors and promise to defend them with his life.

Also noted earlier, the epic *Gilgamesh* of Sumerian origin offers a perfect example. The earliest known poem of its kind, drawn from age-old lore, it recounts the adventures of a man bullied by gods who direct his life and decree that it will cease, though he longs for immortality; in the end, Gilgamesh settles into being the ruler of Uruk, which, it seems, he was made to be. Homer's *Odyssey*, drawn from popular Greek fictions, renders a comparable point by how it has Odysseus wander back to his throne in Ithaca. In addition, the epic tale of Rome's founding, Virgil's *Aeneid*, demonstrates through the protagonist's refusal of love from Dido and his rush to war against Turnus that fortunes are directed by outside authorities. Springing from the territory around the fabled city of Timbuktu, *Sundiata* reveals how the title character fulfills his lot to father the Malian empire by deserting his own welfare in the interest of his country. Finally, *Beowulf* the English epic, based on Scandinavian legends, hailing bravery and kinship, narrates the hero's defeat of Grendel and the dragon to show that everyone's prospects are a matter of prophecy.

By the Age of Reason, Americans were conjuring up images of self-determination as a right. Inspired by maverick thinkers, like Locke, Voltaire, and Rousseau, they figured that they could work as pilots instead of acting as passengers in their lives. The secret weapon to victory, in their view, loomed as knowledge poured into individual heads. They dreamed that everyone arrives with a mind that treated as fertile soil, can free each and all to realize the best of all possible worlds. The community felt tied to an Invisible Hand waiting to help them help themselves to a good life. By civic gauges, being subject to another's will is evil. According to foreign measures, the idea had to inscribe an odd perspective.

Thomas Jefferson was cognizant of the country's moorings. For a friend Henry Lee, he noted the presence of a unifying sense, circulating through his surroundings, stressing equality with a religious fervor. The trend, he told Roger Weightman, disposed the nation to challenge "men" everywhere to break out of the shackles by which societies had bound them to self-denial and to plunge themselves into the boon of self-control. Swayed by the spirit about him, Jefferson felt that the history of all previous cultures was a history of tyranny in which most human beings were treated as if they had been made with leather hides for a handful to ride with boots and spurs. Jefferson's formula for slipping the yoke of the past, which he held sacred to his fellow Americans, amounted to a simple equation pointing to learning as the key to the portal for happiness. A spread of knowledge among his countrymen, Jefferson divulged to John Adams, would provide the best means of promoting and preserving the general welfare.

Adams shared Jefferson's opinion. It is evident in his *Dissertation on the Canon and Feudal Law* (1765). It states that an affinity for freedom launched, guided, and completed the formation of American society. He insists that the ultimate fate of the venture depends on a diffusion of knowledge. Tyranny, he says, never prevailed among educated people. With great conviction, Adams claims that ignorance is liable to breed ruin, but learning is bound to preserve a culture congenial to humanity's betterment.

The evident faith in mental cultivation tilted the land against tales in honor of warriors who wield arms to secure kingdoms. Yet, recollections of solitary figures who have employed their wits to realize their potential were ripe for consumption in every quarter. There hence had dissolved all taste for narratives that start with a statement of purpose, solicit the aid of a muse, and skip into the middle of things, before sliding back and forth in time to salute warfare and the supernatural through a series of catalogs and pageants, as happens in the *Odyssey*, as well as its companions cited earlier, in addition to other ones, including France's *La Chanson de Roland* and Spain's *Cantar de mio Cid*.

John McWilliams discerns in *The American Epic* that a unique outlook propelling the Republic generated "a pressing cultural need" for "some kind of heroic song for the New World" (1989, 1) over two centuries ago. The creation "had to be something other than a Homeric, Virgilian, or Miltonic poem" (2), he says. What would make it distinct would be "an affirmation of essential cultural values" (3) overseeing the whole nation. "I have assumed," he confides, "that, once histories and novels became the dominant literary forms in the 1820s and 1830s, 'the American Epic' was far more likely to be written in prose" (5). In his book, he applauds "the premise of both Lukacs and Bakhtin that, once prose became the dominant literary medium, no poem could any longer do the cultural work . . . required of the epic" (6). McWilliams asks, "Did America provide a heroic fable truly worthy of epic stature" (31)? He replies, Not yet really, and until the real thing comes along Americans will have to make do with books like *The Last of the Mohicans*, *Moby-Dick*, and *Leaves of Grass*.

Along with Nathaniel Hawthorne, who failed to witness any inspiring drama progressing around him on the brink of the Civil War, McWilliams overlooked how escapes from tyranny enabled by learning were due to touch a responsive chord; none could succeed more than a slave narrative could. Ephraim Peabody got it right in his 1849 review of the genre. He attests that one can not find a better model for an American epic than "the adventures of a fugitive slave" (Andrews 1991, 24). The *African* fosters an image of heroism reflecting the American dream of how "men" are made to succeed. It encompasses an epic for an individualistic culture. The Old World habit of having a poet eulogize a legendary cohort could not pass muster in American society. Due to the national mind, rating people born to manage their affairs, a personal account of success alone could display the national spirit in black and white.

Its contours were borrowed from the North African *Confessions of St. Augustine*, which, perhaps, sparked the modern era by inciting introspection. The book's slant favors the sketches of rogues, like *La vida de Lazarillo de Tormes* (1554), that were copies of the *Novela Morisca*, the Moorish genre of gallantry. Still, the depth and breath of Equiano's composition have domestic roots; they reprise folklore. Rendering the text iconic of an advocacy for self-development, the final components set the *African* to speak the American mind. The protagonist connotes Everyman in a style that champions the reigning belief system.

The *African* starts with a humble introduction and a family history that passes into a memory of oppression, from which the hero flees through the use of learning, diligently reaped, to harvest prosperity and lead him to public service. Overall, the ex-slave's personal history paints a picture showing that American society at its best would border a sea of swimmers, self-sustaining people, aiding one another, in lieu of a state synonymous with a wide raft of rowers under the rule of a crusty old salt. Eternal ease would never prevail; circumstances would remain unsettled; without endlessly exercising effort and endurance, one would sink into trouble. Knowledge would make all the difference in the world. The *Autobiography* unfolds in a way that carries a similar motif. But since the *African* appeared in print before Franklin's narrative, Equiano beat him to the punch and earned the right to wear the title: "First Master of the American Epic."

"In the name of humanity," Du Bois sensed, the black experience in American civilization has served as "a concrete test of the underlying principles" of the nation (1996, 107). Seeing blacks operating as exceptions proving the rule in the country, he argued, due to conditioning, "there are to-day no truer exponents of the pure human spirit of the Declaration of Independence" than African Americans (106). As well, it is fitting that Richard Wright called the black experience "the history of men who tried to adjust themselves to a world whose laws, customs, and [weapons] were leveled against them" and added, "The Negro is America's metaphor" (1964, 72). Since the land's gestation, racism has restricted blacks to the bottom of society, and the side effect is a social caste of individuals handed down an automatic affinity for public ideals. Equiano's life in slavery pushed him to fight for freedom. From his fateful kidnapping out of his village to his captivity in the New World, his enslavement made him yearn for relief from oppression; it prepared him for an easy conversion to the faith in human nature current in the land. The tides of his time taught him that the absence of liberty is a terrible thing that corrupts "men." In actuality, like a tune that sounds sweet because "its Air or Genius" agrees with "some Motion, Passion or Affection of the Mind" (Franklin 1987, 425), the notion of justice heralded in American civilization had an air in agreement with Equiano's innermost desire during his days in bondage and mobilized him to speak for the nation by writing about himself.

As Sterling Brown would say, there is a "black" aspect to the *African*. It denies the charge that blacks lack the necessities to manage on their own. Equiano deplores that they have resided at the bottom of society because too many of their fellow citizens have entertained a very low opinion of their intellect and thus have deprived them of fair treatment. His voice approximates a dialect of a tongue in relation to the *Autobiography*. It possesses an accent missing from the white volume. Equiano's story indicates that if the country were to afford black citizens along with everyone else a fair chance to acquire useful knowledge, the entire nation would benefit. It is valid to designate the *African* as a black sound of the American Dream.

Beyond the shadow of a doubt, besides Franklin's *Autobiography*, the *African* endorses the ideological basis for the nation. Again, although the two books differ, the difference between them is not drastic. The *African* is distinguished only by a lament that presumptions against black people have stationed the country's promise beyond their reach. The narrator in the book is a forerunner to the storyteller in Ralph Ellison's famous *Invisible Man* who, after being chased into a basement, decides "to affirm the prin-

ciple on which the country was built and not on the men,"
because, "dreamed into being out of the chaos and darkness of the feudal past," it is "greater than the men, greater
than the numbers and the vicious power and all the meth-
ods used to corrupt its name" here ([1952] 1980, 574).
Throughout the *African*, the national spirit is confirmed
and commended. Equiano's narration suggests that in the
New World a swimming expedition into uncharted waters
is under way, and, while it is a noble venture, it is troubled
by a kind of partiality that has caused poor provisions to be
made for black participation. The narrative objects to
black exclusion from the standard policy for involvement
in the national enterprise that officially requires but an
ability to learn, which is native to all "men."

With an inflection absent from the *Autobiography,*
Equiano's expression of the faith animating the culture
underscores Du Bois's observation that black Americans
have felt submerged in the mainstream, yet separate from
it. Du Bois read the black experience in America as a log of
struggle centering on a mission to unite a divided soul.
Referring to blacks, he wrote in *The Souls of Black Folk*,
"One ever feels his twoness, —an American, a [black]; two
souls, two thoughts, two [tense] strivings; two [contending]
ideals in one dark body, whose dogged strength alone
keeps it from being torn asunder" (1996, 102). In the dilem-
ma, Du Bois spotted a phenomenon that has occurred in
every quarter of the country. It was a millstone around
Henry James's neck that prompted him to assure a friend
that it is not easy being a part of the national development;
living in the land is certain to leave one schizophrenic due
to a gnawing identity crisis. With great assurance, James
insisted that the fact of the matter is very simply that for
citizens in the country to some degree or another "it's a
complex fate . . . and one of the responsibilities it entails
is fighting against a superstitious" worship of Old World
relatives.[2] The burden led Theodore Roosevelt to use the

---

2. Written in an 1872 letter, the quotation is recorded on page 548 in *Bartlett's
Familiar Quotations*, edited by Justin Kaplan (Boston: Little, Brown, 1992).

phrase "hyphenated Americans"[3] to describe people in the country as conflicted constituents of one nation holding many traditions. Living in the land has meant having split loyalties. Everywhere citizens have confronted being torn between two poles, one tribal, the other national.

Since the people who populate the land have roots that reach beyond the nation to shores around the globe, everyone has had questions about how what it means to be an American applies. It has long been a common hazard. For two generations, the Puritan settlers who sailed on the *Arbella* with John Winthrop saw themselves on an errand into the wilderness to establish a new England that would observe Old World rites at their best and teach the older country how to avoid corruption on the loose. Later, the Quakers who migrated to Philadelphia with William Penn doubted having a duty to fixate on the construction of a model English society; instead, they wanted to launch a pioneering enterprise which would be unbound by ancient codes mandating obedience to custom. The stance of the alternative sects captured the poles in American society evolving from the "discovery" of the New World in 1492.

On a figurative and literal level too, covered with a vast diaspora from the four corners of the earth, the social landscape encompasses an expansive range of frontiers and settlements. The citizens break into two separate camps. One involves an identification with the past, and the other an association with the future. The former perspective—call it the "settler" camp—permits very little latitude in attitude; it focuses on ancestor worship and invites circling the wagons, closing ranks, imagining the country as a hapless colony of races born at odds. The converse position, the "pioneer" camp, allows lots of latitude in attitude; it takes custom with a grain of salt as it prefers going by trial and error; it perceives the culture as a spirited initiative ordained to mix diverse individuals into an innovative state. Each camp has held white Anglo-Saxon Protestants, Irish Catholics, Italians, and Jews, with American Indians and Asian Americans, too, not to men-

---

3. See the *Metropolitan Magazine* (October 1915): 7.

tion every other ethnicity. This division was a fact of life for Franklin and Equiano. A formal duality has structurally beleaguered citizens for centuries by tearing them one generation after another between yesterday and tomorrow.

The swim of things has propelled the production of a series of autobiographies that look and sound like the *African*, yet shifts in tone distinguish them. They embark flashing humility on a mission to inspire growth. The texts dig into the roots of their protagonists' family trees, prior to locating their heroes, out on a limb in want of independence. A practical education brings everyone the desired end. Afterward, the heroes lend a hand to help others find the same. The narratives contradict the old Puritan belief in human depravity and destiny. They insist that all "men" are good in nature and only await nurturing to blossom into talented and thriving human beings. All of them collectively resemble successive renditions of a song, stamped by modifications in pitch.

Following in the footsteps of the *African* and the *Autobiography*, Douglass's *American Slave* and Harriet Jacobs's *Slave Girl* stand out as excellent examples of a classic American autobiography with an epic stature in the social order. Equiano's narrative gives credit to verbal and trade skills for his success, and Franklin's story thanks printing and writing for his good fortune. The protagonists in *An American Slave* and *A Slave Girl* are grateful to literacy for their rises in society. Each of the black books, with the white one, has a hero who embodies a New World sense of valor that beckons people to gain enough knowledge to support themselves in the world, as if they were seasoned swimmers in a big sea, changing all the time. The inventions envision a democratic organism overflowing with learning as a natural source of justice. All of the slave narratives look like the *Autobiography*. They sound like it, too, until different tribal issues come into play and differentiate the black memoirs from their white companion.

Diverting from the *Autobiography*, the black books lambaste and lament denials of fair chances for blacks to realize the American Dream due to a heavy dose of bigotry, measuring them in worth less than "men" who are born with a natural means to enjoy freedom through the use of learning. The three black works do not stand alone. Most of the "more than six thousand" slave narratives, up to "the [autobiography] of George Washington Carver, published in 1944" (Starling 1981, 1), accompany them. Related texts include: *A Narrative of the Most Remarkable Particulars in the Life of* James Albert *Ukawsaw Gronniosaw* (1774), *A Narrative of the Life and Adventures of Venture* (1798), *The Life and Religious Experience of Jarena Lee* (1836), *A Narrative of the Adventures and Escape of Moses Roper* (1837), *Memoirs of Elleanor Eldridge* (1843), *Narrative of William Wells Brown* (1847), *Narrative of the Life and Adventures of Henry Bibb* (1849), *The Life of Josiah Henson* (1849), and *Behind the Scenes* (1868) by Elizabeth Keckley. Without exception, the given material recounts a passage to freedom inaugurated and piloted by the use of knowledge. Their voices are colored by indignation and grief at the way in which bias shortchanged black lives in slavery days.

Black books in the tradition extend in time to Booker T. Washington's *Up from Slavery* ([1901] 1995), where it reaches a high point. Born a slave boy, the author recalls, "My life had its beginning in the midst of the most miserable, desolate, and discouraging surroundings" (1). Washington greets de jure liberty at the end of the Civil War, but de facto freedom comes to him a whole lot later as a result of his industry, integrity, and education. For a while, in his youth he is so poor that he has to sleep on the streets of Richmond, Virginia. A meticulous sweeping and cleaning of a classroom at the Hampton Institute, however, earns him admission into the school, which causes him to feel like "one of the happiest souls on earth" (31). His studies prepare him for a liberating career as a teacher and orator; through mastery of the skills, he happily makes himself "of such undeniable value to the community in which he live[s] that the community [can]not dispense with his presence" (118); he assumes stewardship of the Tuskegee Institute and thereby helps blacks to find gainful employment in the wake of the Civil War. While wishing and seeking to see black folks rise by his example, Washington admits that it is a daunting prospect for the average one; he observes:

> The world should not pass judgment upon the Negro, and especially the Negro youth, too quickly or too harshly. The Negro boy has obstacles, [sorrows], and temptations to battle that are little known to those not situated as he is. When a white boy undertakes a task, it is taken for granted that he will succeed. On the other hand, people are usually surprised if the Negro boy does not fail. In a word, the Negro youth starts out with the presumption against him. (21)

Yet and still, he believes, the winds of history blow "in the direction of giving mankind more [genius], more culture, more skill, more liberty, and in the direction of extending more sympathy and more brotherly kindness" (119), and no one can halt their movement; so "the individual who can do something that the world wants done will, in the end, make his way regardless of his race" (91).

Zora Neale Hurston's autobiography entitled *Dust Tracks on a Road* ([1942] 1996), though not a slave narrative, harmonizes with *Up from Slavery* and forms an exemplary novel American epic. It revolves around a love of literature that enables the main character to follow her mother's exhortation to "jump at de sun" (13). During her youth, restrictive racial and sexual codes impose upon her "a stifled longing" (27) to go far. But as books like the *Swiss Family Robinson* and *Gulliver's Travels* interest her more than clothing, she matures into a well-read scholar who goes to Morgan and Barnard College prior to doing anthropological research with Franz Boas in the graduate school at Columbia University. Though, as a consequence of social injustice, before she becomes a successful author, she spends time "in Sorrow's kitchen and lick[s] out all the pots" (227), she keeps the faith that she has "the means at [her] disposal for working out [her own] destiny" (226). She recognizes that racism incites black people to entertain "the gloomy thought that [their numbers] in

America are doomed to be stomped out bodaciously, [if not] shackled to the bottom of things." Subsequently, she remarks about her people that "we will go where the internal drive carries us like everybody else" (192). In light of discerning that "skins were no measure of what was inside people," she notices "no curse in being black" nor any "extra flavor by being white" (191); she expresses certainty that the Creator makes all people one by one rather than in groups and endows everyone with enough good sense to make a way out of no way with the help of learning.

Richard Wright's self-portrait in *Black Boy* (1945) exhibits the same sense of possibility. His private history leads off with him stranded in a world of ignorance, fear, stifled curiosity, brutality, and poverty. Hunger lurks "at [his] elbow when [he] play[s]," and he "wake[s] up at night to find hunger standing at [his] bedside, staring at [him] gauntly" (21); he either obeys white folks and black adults or is punished; in need of solace, he repents, "I was a drunkard in my sixth year, before I had begun school" (29). Taking his own reality as a microcosm for "the essential bleakness of black life," he mourns "that [blacks] had never been [entitled] to [savor] the full spirit of [the West], that they lived somehow in it but not of it" (45). In any event, "glad days" dawn on him and give him "liberty for the free play of impulse and, from anxiety and restraint" (44); he has reading to thank. "It had been my accidental reading of fiction and literary criticism," Wright says, looking back, "that had evoked in [him] vague glimpses of life's [options]" (283); inspired by "Horatio Alger stories," he "[builds] up in [himself] a dream" (186) that has him expect variation, movement, adjustment, and directs him to migrate to the "North, full of a hazy notion that life could be lived with dignity, that the personalities of others should not be violated, that men should be able to confront other men without fear or shame, and that if men were lucky in their living on [earth] they might win some redeeming meaning for their having struggled and suffered here beneath the stars" (285).

The twentieth century has welcomed a good many novel American epics written by African Americans attuned to the rhythm of *Black Boy*. There is the *Big Sea* (1940) by Langston Hughes, which, comparing writing to fishing in the ocean, portrays the poet as a lively spirit who overcomes adversity by falling in love with books. Claude Brown's *Manchild in the Promised Land* (1965), detailing his flight from the horrors of the underclass in Harlem, is a big part of the tradition; *The Autobiography of Malcolm X* (1965), tracing his evolution into a champion for human rights, composes a truly rather impressive statement of the convention. In *Coming of Age in Mississippi* (1968), the illustration of Anne Moody's growth into a Civil Rights activist has a similar effect. It is also true of *I Know Why the Caged Bird Sings* (1968), in which Maya Angelou recalls how books helped her to recover from shock in her girlhood after being raped by her mother's lover; literature frees her to look to the future with hope and sleep untroubled at night. *Crusade for Justice* (1970), a journal of the development of Ida B. Wells into a staunch opponent of lynching, has a thematic content comparable to the motifs in all of the preceding. Recent supplements include *Zami* (1982) by Audre Lorde in front of *Woodholme* (1995) by DeWayne Wickham. Each one of them locates destiny in private hands ready to work well naturally with the aid of skills afforded and acquired.

An endless stream of lives recollected by whites has echoed the sentiments of the black books, speaking for a social order of self-reliant souls. The white works first crested with the publication of Franklin's *Autobiography*. The line of stories reached a high tide with the printing of *Two Years before the Mast* (1840), recording Richard Henry Dana's moral awakening at sea. The *Life of P. T. Barnum* (1855), tracking the showman's crafty rise to prominence, extended the string. With an odd twist, it was lengthened further by *The Education of Henry Adams* (1918), memorializing the Bostonian who drifted from the dictates of custom and determined "the task of education" to be "running order through chaos, direction through space, discipline through freedom, unity through multiplicity" (12) in a dynamic cosmos. The *Autobiography of Andrew Carnegie* (1920) with its gospel about the way to wealth continued the stream next. Every last one of the white male voice airs a supreme confidence that its author's humanity will and should be taken totally for granted.

While narratives by white women have conformed to the convention, doubts raised by sexism about the native capacity of females to perform heroic feats have covered their expressions with a distinct hue. A *Narrative of the Life of Mrs. Mary Jemison* (1824) falls into this category with its ledger of intimate relations with several Native Americans. The bold journey from Boston to New Haven logged in the *Journal of Madam Knight* (1825) resides in the class. A *New England Girlhood* (1889), written by Lucy Larcom dwells there along with Elizabeth Cady Stanton's *Eighty Years and More* (1898), in front of several texts, preceding Annie Dillard's *Pilgrim at Tinker Creek* (1974) and later works. Every one of them attests that the average woman can learn to profit from self-reliance as well as any man. Among them, *Ruth Hall* stands out, though it seems to be something else altogether, since it is masked as fiction.

A compatible testimony resounds in the fluent tale of the voyage made by Mary Antin out of a Russian ghetto into a Boston slum, en route to an education at Barnard, called *The Promised Land* ([1912] 1969). Antin's story clearly reverberates with an advocacy for women's rights in harmony with the hopes for females expressed in the narratives of Jacobs and Fern on top of other women's writings mentioned. As a child, she regrets that there are few avenues to success open to girls in her surroundings; it is evident in the absence of a "free school for girls" (26) outside their mothers' kitchens, where they would learn "to bake and cook and manage, to knit, sew, and embroider; also to spin and weave, in country places" (34) for the purpose of becoming a wife to a man. Diligently reading finds, like "Louisa Alcott stories" and "boys' books of adventure, [several] by Horatio Alger" (257), broadens her horizons; the experience sways her to "propose to be [her] own pilot" in life with a resolve that endures "the mists of uncertainty" as well as "the reefs of speculation," steadied by an undying "hope to make port at last" and discover "welcoming faces on the shore" (78). For the benefit of women, an American author has never conceived a "better symbol of the genuine, practical equality," of everyone in the nation and, equally noteworthy, no writer has ever conjured up a more fine memory of "the citizen in the making" (362); in sum, the pitch of the *Promised Land* is an ideal version of the theme in the American epic modulated by a female and an immigrant stress.

The emphasis in the *Promised Land* on the making of an American links it to the *African*, which deals with a conversion "from the Old World with its settled prejudices" (Antin 246) to a social order "pregnant with possibilities" (Antin 358) awaiting wise exploration. Scores of harmonious texts have appeared. They include the *Making of an American* by Jacob Riis (1924), as well as the *Education of Abraham Cahan* (1926). *Barrio Boy* (1971) by Ernesto Galarza has become a member of the group, as has, *America Is in the Heart* (1946), communicating the transformation into an American experienced by Carlos Bulosan, who felt "fortunate to find work in a library and to be close to books" (71), for society was thus prevented from "narrowing" his existence "into an island" (121) of darkness and gloom. They are joined by manuscripts from the children of immigrants with variations in tone indicative of a sense of a division between two poles. Present among them are Monica Sone's *Nisei Daughter* (1953), telling of her ascent from the rut of a Japanese internment camp around World War II, and *Down These Mean Streets* (1967) about how learning to write permitted Piri Thomas to release himself from a cycle of crime and custody. While disguised as pure fiction like *Ruth Hall*, Maxine Hong Kingston's *Woman Warrior* (1976) counts as an epic expression with a second-generational accent, apparent in *An Ethnic at Large* (1978) by Jerre Mangione where the author spies a considerable distance between his "Sicilian and American worlds" (32), which he has to face ahead of initiating a brilliant career out of Syracuse University culminating in a weekend stay as a guest of honor at the White House. Richard Rodriguez's *Hunger of Memory* (1981) works pretty much the same.

Every imaginable sort of citizen has had a hand in the cultivation of the literary practice. Native Americans have contributed to the convention differently the same as everyone else. In 1829, William Apess published *A Son of the Forest*; a few nominal, geographical, and adjectival amendments would render the book a dead ringer for a slave narrative on par with *An American Slave*. Apess opens his story with a humble introduction, stating that he considers himself, like all "men," an heir to "one great progenitor—Adam" and therefore really "nothing more than a worm of the earth." He notes that his father was mixed of white and red blood, but his mother was a Pequot "in whose veins a single drop of the white man's blood never flowed" (4). Orphaned and sold into indentured servitude, he runs away, joins the New York militia, and acts as a drummer boy in the War of 1812, after gaining religious instruction in the Methodist faith, calculating "that I could take care of myself and get my own living," and determining "to be a man—*to do business for myself and become rich*" (14). While his wishes seem illusory for a time as he falls victim to a rum addiction, in due course, he converts from a rogue to a missionary among his people and contests for their human rights. In the end, Apess's story recommends the spread of learning in the interest of the general welfare.

The oldest extant Native American autobiography is a brief sketch that was first published in 1762. Written by Samson Occom, it is entitled "A Short Narrative of My Life." Later, during 1824, a Cherokee woman issued her *Memoirs of Catherine Brown,* meriting inclusion here. Another good text that has materialized is *Life among the Piutes* (1883) by Sarah Winnemucca Hopkins. Luther Standing Bear's *My Indian Boyhood* (1931) is a companion piece. It is also true of *From the Deep Woods to Civilization* (1916), by Charles Alexander Eastman, antecedent to *Lakota Woman* (1990) by Mary Crow Dog. Each narrative depicts knowledge as power.

Every private history to which this study refers pens a strain of a narrative flood predicated on a solitary theme. The lot centers on a figure who flees a terrible past through schooling and finds a better life that leads to public service. Each and all reflect talk about human nature that has set national sights. Within the country, the writings form editions of an epic, novel in history. One could regard all of them as imitation slave narratives; a more classic type has yet to appear. But other versions are just as ideal in their own ways. In unison, they call for an exceptional order that urges people to accept that they have the power to sink or swim on their own in a shifting universe with acquired skill. In many tones, together they hail the American Dream.

An exclusive clan in the country has never alone had a mind to speak for the nation by telling a tale of liberation wrung from tyranny through individual toil. Ethnocentrism has obscured the truth time and again. A global sense of history and literature paired with a feel for celebrated American autobiographies composed over the centuries acts as an antidote for mistrusting that every manner of citizen has shared and shaped a stream of thought, circumscribing the culture's drift and inclining inhabitants to embrace a novel story of epic import within the national sweep, recounting a passage to freedom in which learning looms as a ladder to a lofty perch reachable with resolution by everyone. On different frequencies, a common social channel has carried flocks of denizens in the country. The result is a literary convention of recorded lives that harbors disparate voices.

Postscript

One spring Saturday in the 1960s, when I was still small enough to ride the municipal bus line for free, I took a long walk with my mother from our Philadelphia rowhouse to the Free Library branch, more than a good mile from our neighborhood. The trip got me my first library card and turned up my earliest idols. In truth, it set me on a course that drove me to see industry, integrity, and intelligence as the keys to success.

Inside the cool building, clothed in a mismatched, thrift-shop, shirt-and-pants outfit, I gawked at people from all walks of life with their heads buried in books. While I stood about the registration counter, my mother signed me up for a borrower's card. After that, she took me by the hand to the children's area. Along the way, she convinced me that we were on a treasure hunt to unearth goods more precious than gold. A flood of excitement washed all over me. Once in the children's section, my mother left me to go it alone, so that she could find herself a book, and I could learn to choose for myself.

At first, I was nervous on my own. I could not imagine how to proceed. Luckily, I received a hand from a white lady. She was a nice librarian who directed me to several shelves, through which I combed with wide eyes until I dug up a bunch of illustrated storybooks, including primers on Benjamin Franklin, Abraham Lincoln, and

George Washington Carver. Firmly, I clung to them, for they were about poor boys who had found better lives for themselves, and I wished for a way to do likewise.

As I made up my mind about the books that I would take home, I pressed them to my side and, according to plan, went to wait in the lobby for my mother. In minutes, she appeared, smiling, with *Yes, I Can!*, the autobiography of Sammy Davis, Jr., a best-seller that she had been dying to read, tightly wrapped in her arms. I was happy to see her mostly due to the fact that I could hardly put off exploring my finds. We could never have gotten home soon enough for me. Very much, I resented walking back. I wanted to hop on the bus in order to speed up the trip. But I bit my tongue and stayed the course.

Any other Saturday, I would have been delighted to stop at our neighborhood soul-food shack to carry out fried-fish dinners. But I was not for it on that day. I wondered why we even had to bother. I felt that in my hands I was holding vital secrets about which I hungered to learn. Food counted as the least of my concerns.

After what seemed like an eternity, we returned to our rowhouse. I immediately tore into my books. I did not leave a page unturned in a single one. It was magical. The primers inspired me to believe that I could rise from rags to riches if I devoted myself to honesty, diligence, and learning.

My experience misfits the stereotype perpetuated by Lino Graglio, the University of Texas law professor who contends that black childhoods routinely leave children too uncaring to compete on a level playing field in schools. I was not raised to shun ambition, as the instructor implies. My youth taught me that success depends on preparation within the grasp of each and all.

Through parental guidance, I picked Franklin, Lincoln, and Carver as role models. They never strayed very far from my mind. Thoughts of Franklin especially consumed me after my mother ushered me through the city institute for science bearing his name, on the parkway toting his title, too. He became most special, for he was a local legend. In my hometown, Franklin had managed to flee poverty and realize prosperity by learning all that he could, then putting the information to good use. Seeing that made me determined to follow in his footsteps.

I closeted my respect for Franklin to be politically correct in the rising black nationalist movement to which I subscribed at the end of the 1960s. Ironically, though, through the habit of reading, I uncovered black champions, on top of Carver, such as Frederick Douglass, Richard Wright, and Claude Brown, who, like Franklin, utilized study and spunk to better themselves. Their stories served to justify my regard for Franklin. Keeping his success in mind, I developed a confidence in knowledge as power. It guided me into the University of Pennsylvania.

On my own and in need of a job right away so that I could afford to keep paying the rent for a room-and-a-half, third-floor walk-up off a city park, I dropped out of Penn in 1976 ready to take any job and parlay it into a career that would emulate the success of my heroes. That summer, I made ends meet by working daily as a tour guide at the Living History Center under the auspices of the Bicentennial Corporation. But the company downsized and dropped my position in the fall.

Since the Christmas shopping season was around the corner, I knew that department stores needed to expand their sales forces. So, after a week of dieting on grits to save carfare for job-hunting, I talked my way into a chance to sell men's budget sportswear in the basement of a major store. I swore to myself that I would soar to the top of the company.

Mixing and matching a wardrobe of two jackets, three pants, four ties, and five shirts to look presentable, I rode the bus to work, full of pride, with a book and a brown-bag lunch in tow. From the instant that I went on the clock until the second that I came off it, with my sleeves rolled up, I worked hard. My performance left my superiors very impressed. By the middle of January, they had me in a management training program, by the end of March, they had me assisting their top buyer, and by the beginning of the next year, they had me to thank for record sales in the men's clothing division.

While I was in training, top store executives had assured my class that everyone who finished the program would get an equal opportunity to pursue any part of the business that proved interesting. Thereafter, as I studied sales promotion, I grew excited about advertising. It blew my mind to have my bid for a spot in the marketing office rejected out of hand. The managing director of the unit held that I lacked the qualifications. A white kid right out of college got to fill the vacancy that I coveted.

In retrospect, I realize that my expectations crashed into a glass ceiling. It left me very sore. My ambition flew out the window. Unwilling to continue working, I quit and cast in my lot with others whose spirits were deflated by shattered dreams. I ended up adrift in the smog and sprawl of Los Angeles.

Bumming around the oceanfront in Venice Beach between temporary jobs, I started reading a lot to pass time. It proved to be a worthwhile diversion, particularly since it led me to reread Ralph Ellison's *Invisible Man*. The novel, beginning where it ends, like a boomerang, returning to its source, permitted me to put my experience into perspective. It struck me as a caricature of my own history. Reviewing its account of the venture to rise in the land that strands the hero in an old hidden basement, I saw that though blacks, like me, have been swimming in the same stream of consciousness that swayed Franklin, color prejudice has motivated our fellow Americans to discount our potential; it has blinded them to our humanity. Among blacks, the result is an ironic population ever prone to seek Franklin's sort of success but checked at each and every turn by a base fiction that reserves the American Dream, for whites only!

My story is a testament to the charm of the tradition treated in the foregoing text. Fueled by the national spirit authorizing the convention at issue, my life blasted off its launch pad with a rather ideal trajectory. It arched from poverty and ran toward prosperity. Wrongfully, however, racial discrimination dipped it down and provoked it to stray. Had I never swam in the mainstream, I would have sunk into defeat. My upbringing kept hope alive in the depths of my soul. So, after a two-year sojourn, I vacated the City of Angels and went back to Penn in the City of Brotherly Love, where I stayed as a student until I earned a Ph.D. in English. Now, a professor at Temple University, I teach undergraduates about African American autobiography, and I refer to my own experience in classes to highlight the writing's pull over the land.

Sources

Adams, Charles Francis. *Richard Henry Dana*. Boston, MA: Houghton, Mifflin, 1890.

Adams, Henry. *The Education of Henry Adams*. Boston, MA: Houghton, Mifflin, [1918] 1973.

Adams, John. *Dissertation on the Canon and Feudal Law*. In *Political Writings of John Adams*, edited by George A. Peek. Indianapolis: Bobbs-Merrill, [1765] 1954.

Andrews, William, ed. *Critical Essays on Frederick Douglass*. Boston: G. K. Hall, 1991.

_____. *To Tell a Free Story*. Champaign-Urbana: University of Illinois Press, 1986.

Antin, Mary. *The Promised Land*. Princeton: Princeton University Press, [1912] 1969.

Apess, William. *A Son of the Forest*. In *On Our Own Ground*. Edited by Barry O'Connell. Amherst: University of Massachusetts Press, [1829] 1992.

Aptheker, Herbert. *Essays in the History of the American Negro*. New York: International Publishers, 1964.

_____. *The Negro People in the United States*. New York: Citadel, 1951.

Aristotle. *The Politics of Aristotle*. New York: Oxford University Press, [original publication date unknown] 1971.

Augustine, Saint. *The Confessions of Saint Augustine*. Garden City: Image Books, [ca. 400] 1960.

Baker, Houston A. *The Journey Back*. Chicago: University of Chicago Press, 1980.

_____. *Long Black Song*. Charlottesville: University Press of Virginia, 1972.

Bakhtin, M. M. *The Dialogic Imagination*. Austin: University of Texas Press, 1981.

Baldwin, James. *Notes of a Native Son*. Boston: Beacon Press, 1983.

Barton, Rebecca Chalmers. *Witnesses for Freedom*. New York: Harper and Row, 1948.

Barzun, Jacques. *Race: A Study in Modern Superstition*. New York: Harcourt Brace, 1937.

Baym, Nina. *Women's Fiction*. Ithaca, NY: Cornell University Press, 1978.

Bennett, Lerone. *Before the Mayflower*. New York: Penguin Books, [1962] 1984.

Blassingame, John. *The Slave Community*. New York: Oxford University Press, 1979.

Blassingame, John W., and John R. McKivigan. *The Frederick Douglass Papers*. Vol. 5. New Haven: Yale University Press, 1992.

Boelhower, William. *Immigrant Autobiography in the United States*. Verona, Italy: Essedue, 1982.

Bontemps, Arna. "The Slave Narrative: An American Genre." In *Great Slave Narratives*, edited by Bontemps. Boston: Beacon Press, 1969.

Brawley, Benjamin, ed. *Early Negro American Writer*. New York: Dover, [1935], 1970.

Braxton, Joanne. *Black Women Writing Autobiography*. Philadelphia: Temple University Press, 1989.

Brown, Sterling. "Introduction to the *Negro Caravan*." New York: Arno Press, 1969.

Brumble, H. David. *American Indian Autobiography*. Berkeley: University of California Press, 1988.

Bruss, Elizabeth. *Autobiographical Acts*. Baltimore: Johns Hopkins University Press, 1976.

Bulosan, Carlos. *America Is in the Heart*. Seattle: University of Washington Press, [1946] 1990.

Butcher, Margaret Just. *The Negro in American Culture*. New York: Knopf, [1956] 1972.

Butterfield, Stephen. *Black Autobiography in America*. Amherst: University of Massachusetts Press, 1974.

Carby, Hazel. *Reconstructing Womanhood*. New York: Oxford University Press, 1987.

Cervantes, Miguel de. *Don Quixote*. New York: Norton, [1605] 1981.

Cixous, Helene. "The Laugh of the Medusa." Translated by Keith Cohen and Paula Cohen. *Signs* 1 (Summer 1976).

Clark, John H. "The Origin and Growth of Afro-American Literature." In *Black Voices*. New York: Mentor Books, 1968.

Cooley, Thomas. *Educated Lives*. Columbus: The Ohio State University Press, 1976.

Sources   **149**

Cox, James M. *Recovering Literature's Lost Ground*. Baton
    Rouge: Louisiana State University Press, 1989.
Crevecoeur, St. John de. *Letters from an American Farmer*.
    Edited by Albert Stone. New York: Penguin Books,
    [1782] 1986.
Dana, Richard Henry. *Two Years before the Mast*. New York:
    Penguin, [Harper and Brothers, 1840] 1986.
Davis, Angela. *Women, Race, and Class*. New York: Vintage
    Books, 1983.
Davis, David Brion. *The Problem of Slavery in Western Culture*.
    Ithaca, NY: Cornell University Press, 1966.
Defoe, Daniel. *Robinson Crusoe*. New York: Penguin, [1719]
    1983.
Dinnerstein, Leonard. *Native and Strangers*. New York: Oxford
    University Press, 1990.
Douglass, Frederick. *Narrative of the Life of Frederick Douglass,
    An American Slave*. New York: Bedford, [1845] 1993.
Du Bois, W.E.B. *The Oxford W.E.B. Du Bois Reader*. Edited
    by Eric Sunquist. New York: Oxford University Press,
    1996.
Dudley, David. *My Father's Shadow*. Philadelphia: University
    of Pennsylvania Press, 1992.
Ellison, Ralph. *Invisible Man*. New York: Vintage Books,
    [1952] 1980.
Emerson, Ralph Waldo. *Essays and Lectures*. New York:
    Library of America, 1983.
Equiano, Olaudah. *The Interesting Narrative of the Life of
    Olaudah Equiano . . . the African*. New York: Bedford,
    [1789] 1995.
Fern, Fanny. *Ruth Hall*. New York: Penguin, [1855] 1997.
Filler, Louis. *The Crusade against Slavery*. New York: Harper,
    1960.
Foster, Frances Smith. *Witnessing Slavery*. Madison: Univer-
    sity of Wisconsin Press, [Greenwood, 1979] 1994.
Franklin, Benjamin. *The Autobiography of Benjamin Franklin*.
    New York: Bedford, [1791] 1993.
_____. *Benjamin Franklin, Writings*. New York: Library of
    America, 1987.
Franklin, H. Bruce. *The Victim as Criminal and Artist*. New
    York: Oxford University Press, 1978.
Gates, Henry Louis. *The Signifying Monkey*. New York: Oxford
    University Press, 1988.
Gayle, Addison. *The Black Aesthetic*. Garden City, NY: Double
    day, 1971.
Gilman, Richard. *The Confusion of Realms*. New York: Random
    House, 1969.
Guillen, Claudio. *Literature as System*. Princeton: Princeton
    University Press, 1971.

Harris, Susan K. *19th-Century American Women's Novels*. New York: Cambridge University Press, 1990.

Hawthorne, Nathaniel. *Letters of Hawthorne to William D. Ticknor*. Vol. 1. Newark, NJ: Carteret Book Club, 1910.

hooks, bell. *Ain't I a Woman*. Boston: South End Press, 1982.

Hurston, Zora Neale. *Dust Tracks on a Road*. New York: HarperCollins, [1942] 1996.

Jacobs, Harriet. *Incidents in the Life of a Slave Girl*. New York: Harcourt Brace Jovanovich, [1861] 1973.

Jefferson, Thomas. *Writings*. New York: Library of America, 1984.

Jelinek, Estelle. *Women's Autobiography*. Bloomington: Indiana University Press, 1980.

Jordan, Winthrop. *White over Black*. Baltimore: Penguin, 1969.

Karcher, Carolyn L. *Shadow over the Promised Land*. Baton Rouge: Louisiana State University Press, 1980.

Kramnick, Isaac, ed. *The Portable Enlightenment*. New York: Penguin, 1995.

Kristeva, Julia. *The Kristeva Reader*. Edited by Toril Moi. New York: Columbia University Press, 1986.

Lawrence, D.H. *Studies in Classic American Literature*. New York: The Viking Press, [1923] 1964.

Lopez, Claude-Anne, and E. Herbert. *The Private Franklin*. New York: Norton, 1975.

Mailer, Norman. "The White Negro." From *Advertisements for Myself*. New York: Putnam, 1959.

Mangione, Jerre. *An Ethnic at Large*. Philadelphia: University of Pennsylvania Press, [1942] 1983.

Martin, Jane Roland. *Reclaiming a Conversation*. New Haven, CT: Yale University Press, 1985.

Matthiessen, F. O. *American Renaissance*. New York: Oxford University Press, 1941.

McMichael, George, ed. *Anthology of American Literature*. New York: Macmillan, 1974.

McWilliams, John. *The American Epic: Transforming a Genre, 1770-1860*. New York: Cambridge University Press, 1989.

Melville, Herman. *Moby Dick*. New York: Holt, Rinehart, and Winston, [1851] 1964.

Nash, Gary, and Jean Soderlund. *Freedom by Degrees*. New York: Oxford University Press, 1991.

Niane, D. T. *Sundiata*. London: Longman, 1993.

Olney, James. *Metaphors of Self*. Princeton: Princeton University Press, 1972.

O'Meally, Robert G. "Frederick Douglass' 1845 *Narrative*." In *Afro-American Literature*, edited by Dexter Fisher and Robert Stepto. New York: Modern Language Association, 1979.

Padilla, Genaro. *My History, Not Yours*. Madison: University of Wisconsin Press, 1993.

Pattee, Fred Lewis. *The Feminine Fifties*. New York: D. Appleton-Century, 1940.

Patterson, Orlando. *Freedom*. New York: BasicBooks, 1991.

Peterson, Merrill. *The Portable Thomas Jefferson*. New York: Penguin, 1981.

Plato. *The Republic*. Indianapolis: Hackett, [@380 B.C.] 1992.

Porter, Dorothy. *Early Negro Writing*. Boston: Beacon, 1971.

Preston, Dickson J. *Young Frederick Douglass*. Baltimore: Johns Hopkins University Press, 1980.

Quarles, Benjamin. *The Negro in the Making of America*. New York: Collier Books, 1987.

Ravitch, Diane. *The American Reader*. New York: Harper Collins, 1990.

Redding, J. Saunders. *To Make a Poet Black*. Chapel Hill: University of North Carolina Press, 1939.

Roberts, J. M. *History of the World*. New York: Oxford University Press, 1993.

Rossi, Alice S. *The Feminist Papers*. Boston: Northeastern University Press, 1988.

Rousseau, Jean-Jacques. *Emile; ou De l'education*. New York: Basic Books, [1762] 1979.

Sayre, Robert. "The Proper Study." In *American Autobiography*, edited by Albert Stone. Englewood Cliffs, NJ: Prentice-Hall, 1981.

Schneir, Miriam. *Feminism: The Essential Historical Writings*. New York: Vintage Books, 1972.

Shea, D. *Spiritual Autobiography in Early America*. Princeton: Princeton University Press, 1968.

Showalter, Elaine. *A Literature of Their Own*. Princeton: Princeton University Press, 1977.

Smith, Barbara. "Toward a Black Feminist Criticism." *Conditions: Two* 1, no. 2 (October 1977).

Smith, Sidonie. *Where I'm Bound*. Westport, CT: Greenwood Press, 1974.

Smith, Valerie. *Self-Discovery and Authority in Afro-American Narrative*. Cambridge: Harvard University Press, 1987.

Smith-Rosenberg, C. "The Female World of Love and Ritual." *Signs* 1 (Autumn 1975).

Spacks, Patricia Meyer. *The Female Imagination*. New York: Knopf, 1975.

Starling, Marion Wilson. *The Slave Narrative: Its Place in American History*. Boston: G. K. Hall, 1981.

Stepto, Robert. "Narration, Authentication, and Authorial Control in Frederick Douglass's *Narrative* of 1845." In *Afro-American Literature*, edited by Dexter Fisher and Robert Stepto. New York: Modern Language Association, 1979.

Tocqueville, Alexis de. *Democracy in America*. Vols. 1, 2. New York: Alfred A. Knopf, [1835, 1840] 1963.

Tolles, Frederick B., ed. *The Witness of William Penn*. New York: Macmillan, 1957.

Turner, Frederick Jackson. *The Frontier in American History*. New York: Holt, 1920.

Turner, Lorenzo D. *Anti-Slavery Sentiment in American Literature prior to 1865*. Washington, DC: Association for the Study of Negro Life and History, 1929.

Walker, Alice. "In Search of Our Mothers' Gardens." *Ms.* (May 1974).

Walker, Nancy. *Fanny Fern*. New York: Twayne, 1993.

Warren, Joyce W. *The (Other) American Traditions*. New Brunswick, NJ: Rutgers University Press, 1993.

_____. ed. *Ruth Hall and Other Writings*. New Brunswick, NJ: Rutgers University Press, 1986.

Washington, Booker T. *Up from Slavery*. New York: Oxford University Press, [1901] 1995.

Wells, H. G. *An Outline of History*. New York: Garden City Books, 1961.

Welter, Barbara. *Dimity Convictions*. Athens: Ohio University Press, 1976.

Whitman, Walt. *Song of Myself*. In *The Norton Anthology of American Literature*, edited by Nina Baym. New York: Norton, [1881] 1998.

Williams, Kenny J. *They Also Spoke*. Nashville: Townsend Press, 1970.

Wollstonecraft, Mary. *Vindication of the Rights of Woman*. New York: Penguin, [1792] 1975.

Woodson, Carter G. *The Mis-education of the Negro*. Washington, D.C.: Associated Publishers, 1933.

Wright, Richard. *Black Boy*. New York: Harper and Row, 1945.

____. *White Man Listen!* New York: Doubleday, 1964.

Yellin, Jean Fagan, ed. *Incidents in the Life of a Slave Girl, Written by Herself*. Cambridge: Harvard University Press, 1987.

Index

Adams, Abigail, 27, 57, 107
Adams, Henry, 135
Adams, John, 57, 125
Aeneid, xiii, 4-5, 124
Alger, Horatio, 98, 99, 136
Angelou, Maya, 135
Antin, Mary, 136-37
Apess, William, 138
Aptheker, Herbert, 27, 74
Aristotle, 14, 86, 87
Attucks, Crispus, 28

Baba, Ahmed, 77, 121
Baker, Houston, 46, 47, 52
Bakhtin, Mikhail, 6
Baldwin, James, 117-18
Banneker, Benjamin, 31
Barton, Rebecca Chalmers, 48
Barzun, Jacques, 121
Baym, Nina, 111
Beecher, Catherine, 80
Benezet, Anthony, 37, 58
Beowulf, 12
Bernal, Martin, 16n
black art, 47
black studies, 12, 46
Blassingame, John, 70-71
Bohannon, Paul, 76n
Bontemps, Arna, 47
Braxton, Joanne, 98
Brown, Claude, 135, 143

Brown, Sterling, xiii, 128
Brown, William Wells, 42
Bulosan, Carlos, 137
Butcher, Margaret J., 47, 117
Butterfield, Stephen, 46

Cahan, Abraham, 137
Carnegie, Andrew, 136
Carby, Hazel, 90
Carver, George Washington, 132, 142
Civil rights, 47, 56
Civil War, 42, 56, 59, 60
Cixous, Helene, 96
classic slave narratives, 132
Columbian Orator, The, 66
Columbus, Christopher, 22, 120
Cox, James, 43, 49

Dana, Richard Henry, xiii, 2, 8, 41, 50-52, 63-65
Davis, Angela, 93
de Crevecoeur, St. John, 24, 44
de Tocqueville, Alexis, 62-63
Dillard, Annie, 136
Dinnerstein, Leonard, 26n
Diop, Cheikh Anta, 16n
Divina Commedia, 5
Don Quixote, 76, 116

Douglass, Frederick, xiii, 2, 8,
    41, 52-56, 65-68, 70-
    73, 85, 113
Du Bois, W. E. B., 119, 127,
    129
Dumas, Alexander, 77, 122

Egypt, 3, 74, 76n, 77n, 87, 121
Ellison, Ralph, 128, 144
Emerson, Ralph Waldo, 60,
    61, 69
Equiano, Olaudah, xiii, 9-11,
    17-19, 28-30, 32-36,
    54, 99, 113, 127

Faerie Queene, 5
Fern, Fanny, xiii, 2, 8, 42, 79,
    80-82, 89-90, 97-102
Forten, Sarah, 109
Foster, Frances Smith, 42n,
    98
Franklin, Benjamin, xii, 7, 19-
    21, 25-26, 36-39, 44,
    64, 68, 105, 113, 141,
Franklin, H. Bruce, 52
Fuller, Margaret, 58, 69, 108

Galarza, Ernesto, 137
Garrison, William Lloyd, 42,
    59
Gates, Henry Louis, 46, 75
Gayle, Addison, 46, 47
Gilgamesh, 3-4, 124
Graglio, Lino, 142
Grant, Ulysses S., xi, 7
Guillen, Claudio, 68

Hall, Prince, 28
Harper, Frances, 108
Harris, Susan, 88
Hawkins, John, 13
Hawthorne, Nathaniel, 42,
    54n, 111, 112, 126
Henry, Patrick, 96, 97
Henson, Josiah, 42
Herbert, Eugenia, 19n
Hickey, Dennis, 16n
hooks, bell, 94

Hopkins, Sarah Winnemucca,
    138
Hume, David, 30
Hurston, Zora Neale, 133-34

Iliad, 49

Jacobs, Harriet, xiii, 2, 7, 8,
    79, 83-86, 90-93, 102-5
James, George, 76n
James, Henry, 130
Jefferson, Thomas, 10, 22-23,
    27, 31, 58-59, 117, 125
Jelinek, Estelle, 98
Jordan, Winthrop, 31n, 76n

Keckley, Elizabeth, 109
Kingston, Maxine Hong, 137
Kristeva, Julia, 96

Larcom, Lucy, 136
Lawrence, D. H., 44, 49
Lee, Jarena, 108
Lee, Robert E., xi
Lincoln, Abraham, 7, 60, 141
Lopez, Claude-Anne, 19n
Lorde, Audre, 135
Lucid, Robert Francis, 43
Lundy, Benjamin, 56

Mailer, Norman, 119
Malcolm X, 135
Mangione, Jerre, 137-38
Mann, Horace, 43, 60-61
Matthiessen, F. O., 42
Mayflower, 26
Melville, Herman, 43, 44, 60,
    126
Moody, Anne, 135
Mott, Lucretia, 57, 58

Nash, Gary, 19n

Occom, Samson, 138
Odyssey, xiii, 4, 49, 124
O'Meally, Robert, 47

Paradise Lost, 6
Patterson, Orlando, 14-16
Peabody, Ephraim, 49
Penn, William, 21-22, 58, 130
Pennsylvania Gazette, 20
Philadelphia, 19, 21, 39, 60, 84, 130
Plato, 14, 105
Poor Richard's Almanac, 25
Powell, Colin, 13
Pushkin, Alexander, 77, 122

Quarles, Benjamin, 18, 47, 58

Redding, J. Saunders, 47
Riis, Jacobs, 137
Robinson Crusoe, 6, 19, 100, 105, 116
Rodriguez, Richard, 138
Rogers, Joel A., 76n, 122n
Roosevelt, Theodore, 129-30
Roper, Moses, 42
Rousseau, Jean-Jacques, 106

St. Augustine, 76, 77, 116, 122, 127
Sayre, Robert, 115, 116
Sedgwick, Catherine Maria, 80
Seneca Falls, 57, 94
Sertima, Ivan Van, 76n
Sewall, Samuel, 58
Shakespeare, William, 77n
Showalter, Elaine, 96
Sigourney, Lydia, 80
Smith, Barbara, 96
Smith, Susan Belasco, 81
Smith, Valerie, 93
Smith-Rosenberg, Carroll, 96
Snowden, Frank, 16n, 76n
Soderlund, Jean, 19n
Sone, Monica, 137
Spacks, Patricia Meyer, 96
Stanton, Elizabeth Cady, 57, 58, 98, 108
Stepto, Robert B., 47, 73
Stewart, Maria, 108

Stowe, Harriet Beecher, 42n, 60, 119
Sundiata, 5, 11, 124

Terence, 77, 122
Thomas, Paine, 7
Thomas, Piri, 137
Thoreau, Henry David, 42, 59
Transcendentalism, 61
Truth, Sojourner, 108
Turner, Frederick Jackson, 44
Turner, Nat, 59

Vaughan, Benjamin, 26

Walker, Alice, 96
Walker, David, 73
Warner, Susan, 42, 112
Warren, Joyce, 81, 82n, 90, 97, 98n
Washington, Booker T., xii, 132-33
Washington, George, 7, 59
Wells, H. G., 14, 15, 16n
Wells, Ida B., 135
Whitman, Walt, 61-62, 126
Whittier, John Greenleaf, 59
Wickham, Dewayne, 135
Williams, Charlie, xi-xiii
Williams, Kenny, 48
Willis, Sara Payson, 80
Wollstonecraft, Mary, 105-106
Woolman, John, 33, 58
Wright, Richard, 127, 134, 143
Wylie, Kenneth, 16n

Yellin, Jean Fagan, 85, 110
Yes, I Can!, 142

About the Author

ROLAND L. WILLIAMS, JR. is Assistant Professor of English at Temple University and has published poetry, fiction, and book reviews. He has previously taught at Ohio State University, Otterbein College, and the University of Delaware.

ISBN 0-313-30585-4

90000>

EAN

9 780313 305856

HARDCOVER BAR CODE